Tomas Nesnidal

YOU ARE love

How To Be Loved More, Feel Worthy Of Love, And Live From True Love Every Day

YouAreLovePublishing.com

You Are Love Publishing Ltd.
ISBN 978-1-9993302-0-0 Paperback
ISBN 978-1-9993302-1-7 eBook

YOU ARE LOVE

How To Be Loved More, Feel Worthy Of Love, And Live From True Love Every Day

TOMAS NESNIDAL

TABLE OF CONTENTS

PART I: REALIZE

TABLE OF CONTENTS

PART II: THE 'YOU ARE LOVE' PROCESS

PART III: LIVE & GIVE

AUTHOR'S NOTE

DISCLAIMER: This book will seriously challenge your heart!

Dear Reader,

This is *not* your ordinary reference book. You did not attract it to your life just to "check things out." Synchronicity brought these pages before you for a very serious reason: your heart and your soul are strongly calling for more love in your life—and they won't stop until they succeed.

While your emotional and spiritual needs have attracted the solution, however, your mind has yet to acknowledge any "problem." This means that you will need a real *commitment* to accompany your reading. Realization of the love you already are is waiting for you, but it will only meet you exactly where and when you are ready meet it.

Realization of the love you already are is waiting for you, but it will only meet you exactly where and when you are ready meet it.

Only you can bring yourself to this point. But I am here to help you move toward acceptance of that love—to experience all of its beauty and perfection, and to start truly living from it.

To do that, I must challenge you to open your heart fully and unconditionally, with courage and authenticity. Without an opened heart, the love you already are cannot flow.

So, to help you connect with that courage and live from that commitment, I have prepared five agreements that I want you to make with yourself before you continue. These agreements are here for *YOU*. Think of them as though YOU had written them for YOURSELF.

When you make a personal pact, you are more likely to follow through. After all, you are the one with everything to gain. So, please, read these agreements carefully, and promise yourself that you'll follow them to the letter as you experience this book.

Here they are: the heart-generated agreements given to YOU from YOU.

Agreement I: I will read this book with my HEART, not my brain.

Notice that this book is called, "You are love," not, "You are brain." That's because it was written directly from the heart, intending to reach another heart. Although a lot of "thinking" went into expressing these concepts, they were derived from a place of pure love. In fact, I could only write this when I became highly connected to heart and to the love I already am.

So if you want to really "get" this book, that's where you need to start: in your heart. Open your heart as much as you can, right now. This will accelerate your journey through awakening, realization, and the give and take of pure love.

Agreement II: I will not conceptualize, intellectualize, label, or compare.

This will put you in the moment. Much of what you read here will conflict with "normal" and generally accepted social conventions. That's because love and heart "see" thing differently than logic and brain. Love is more than, separate from, and above concepts.

Putting labels and intellectual constraints on love will not get you too far. You will stay in the same mind bubble, and your life will stay the same. Love cannot be truly realized from the place of mind and thoughts. It can only be realized from the heart.

Agreement III: I will stop making ANY excuses.

One of the reasons why people do not recognize the love they already are is that most of us rely on excuses. Are you one of them? You may place a higher priority on external things. But the funny part is, you go through your day, doing all the things you think are important, for the same reason—to experience and realize more love.

The difference is that those things are not leading anywhere! Otherwise, you wouldn't be reading this book.

So, stop making excuses.

Give yourself permission to ditch the "no time" excuse. It is just a habit, nothing more. Resolve to actually practice what I will ask you to practice in this book, and you will COMMIT yourself to this journey. Just take this simple step. If you don't, nothing will ever change.

Agreement IV: I will make an effort to consciously love myself as I read this book.

Many people hold themselves to higher standards than anyone else, and sometimes we go too far. In order to work in concert with, not against, this book, read it with as much self-love as possible. Sticking with Agreement I—reading with heart, not brain—will help you do this.

If self-love is one of your biggest challenges, then enjoy the support of Agreement II—reading without comparing yourself to what you see, which is a brain-driven activity. Just open your heart, relax into it, and try to "feel" the book.

This is a form of self-love too.

Agreement V: I will be patient and passionate.

This is NOT a "consumer's" book.

When you go shopping, all you have to do is open your wallet. If you don't like what you paid for, you return the product. There are no real consequences. But opening a wallet and opening a heart are two very different things. Your heart doesn't care about your consumer's behavior and mentality!

Your heart wants you to be patient and passionate—to traverse a challenging new landscape gently so that your experience aligns with the attitude you bring to it. So, please, do so. Your heart will reward the effort with a swifter realization of the love you already are and the journey will be less bumpy.

*　*　*

If you have been disappointed by your past heart-related experiences or even dismayed by your entire life direction until now, these agreements are a lot to ask for. But I make the request because, with your commitment to letting your heart take the lead, you can see significant improvements in your life very fast. These may include:

- making more authentic connections with other people
- fulfilling your desire for love from within, instead of waiting for someone or something else to do it
- engaging with others on a plane that is more harmonious with the nature of who you truly are.

In this manner, you can free yourself from worrying about what other people think or say about you. You'll recognize your own integrity and stop comparing yourself with others. You'll find it easier to add more intimacy to your life, including sex.

When you allow yourself to shift from just reading to "experiencing" this book, you can make the move from *chasing* love to *living from* love. You will arrive at a completely new way of living, with fewer insecurities, fears, and doubts—and much more laughter, excitement, and passion. Bring yourself closer to that solution by firmly committing to the five agreements between you and you.

> **...make the move from *chasing* love, to *living from* love.**

Then, go back and read them again. You will be well on your way to abandoning the passive, "checking stuff out" attitude of the consumer and embracing active engagement with your entire being, which wants nothing but to bloom, love, and be loved.

I did it. I know you can too. I have absolute faith in you, and I want you to succeed in changing your life.

With love,

Tomas

INTRODUCTION

COULD THIS HAPPEN TO YOU?

Imagine the feeling of being the most unworthy person on this planet.

Ok, now multiply that unworthiness by ten. Pretty heavy, right? Now, multiply it by a hundred. Nearly impossible to imagine, isn't it? Okay. Now multiply that insane, crushing unworthiness by a million.

Still alive?

Congratulations.

Because when I experienced exactly that catastrophic level of unworthiness for the very first time, I didn't think I would survive.

It happened just before I experienced the source of infinite, unconditional love that we all already are for the first time, and I wouldn't wish that unworthiness phase on my worst enemy. The trauma was equal to or worse than a serious car accident! Yet, I went through it, survived, and a whole new reality was opened to me as an incredible reward:

The reality of inner peace, deep self-connection, and unconditional love. This reality is here, with us, all the time—yet we do our best to ignore and avoid it.

Like most people, I did that too. But such denial can be overcome. Let me share with you what happened to me: the story of a man who lived for too long with the wrong partner—a bitch called "Unworthiness." My state of avoidance made it almost impossible for me to divorce her.

* * *

About four years ago, I realized that I pretty much "had it all."

I was a successful company owner—financially secure, debt-free, and recognized as an authority in my field of expertise. I was happily married, living on a sunny beach, healthy, slim, and in great mental and physical condition.

My life was positive and satisfying, comfortable, and perfectly flowing—what many would call tremendously exciting. I had traveled to sixty-four countries, lived in several different areas of the world, and enjoyed unusual activities like learning to fly an airplane and making short movies about my life. It was almost too perfect. You're probably bored just reading about it!

But don't worry. There was an element of my life that was only masquerading as exciting. Omnipresent, waking up with me every single day and dictating the motivation behind my actions was my unseen "partner." And she seemed wonderful: pushing me to constantly be an over-achiever, aiming for even more money, more admiration, and more of a superior life. She was always hungry to push me toward MORE of everything, and her name was…

…UNWORTHINESS.

Yes, she wasn't even a person.

She was just a combination of unending low self-esteem and self-doubts. But she was faithful, being with me 24/7, from my childhood on into adult life. Her company was hard not to notice. Whatever I did, whatever I achieved, she made sure that I felt like it was not ENOUGH. That I was never, ever good enough.

When I won in various competitions, it never felt like enough. In my thirties, my parents always said that whatever I decided to achieve, I did—yet, this never felt like enough. And despite writing two national bestsellers in my field of expertise and being presented on national TV news many times, I still felt like a total failure.

The Unworthiness bitch was always with me, anytime, anywhere.

I admit that ours was probably a *mutual* love for a long time, because that feeling of insignificance was, in fact, the engine behind my success. As long as Unworthiness was there, it was easy to keep achieving. All it took was to let her remind me how undeserving and small and pathetic I was in this world of so many more amazing, successful, and flawless people, and *Voila!* The desire to prove to the entire world my right to existence emerged again!

Fortunately, this all changed four years ago.

One day, out of nowhere, I realized I couldn't go on like that. I felt truly burned out. I had it all, I was living the dream; yet, the bitch was still there, and I somehow didn't like her as much as before.

I gradually saw the relationship between her and me as artificial. Shallow. Inauthentic. Worse, this relationship seemed to be driven by a constant need to fit into some weird, even more artificial, shallow, and inauthentic social matrix—one in which everybody reminds you of how you SHOULD be, how you SHOULDN'T be, what you should HAVE, and how you should BEHAVE. The message is that you are never "enough" if you don't fulfill all of OTHER PEOPLE'S should, shouldn't, must, mustn't, and other ridiculous expectations.

It was like living in some weird kind of prison. I had no idea what was going on, why I didn't feel better once I met all the criteria that I'd been taught to believe were the means to ultimate happiness. I was exhausted. But I sensed that this Unworthiness bitch, which had somehow been implanted in my head, was the key to the problem.

So, one day I woke up and made a decision: ENOUGH.

So, one day I woke up and made a decision:

ENOUGH.

I couldn't go on.

It was time to make some radical change.

And by radical, I meant it literally: either I would get a complete DIVORCE from that monster, or one of us would have to die (meaning, hopefully, HER).

* * *

Of course, I had no idea what to change or where to start.

It is not as easy as signing a few papers in front of an attorney. This bitch seemed determined that she would not divorce me by any means. So, as in most bad marriages, the first phase was a nonstop FIGHT.

I tried all sorts of things to get Unworthiness out of my life. I had been regularly meditating for ten years, so I turned to meditation. I probably didn't have the right focus, because there was no difference. Then I read books about unworthiness, trying to rationalize my way out of it, using affirmations, positive self-talk—techniques that were supposed to produce a rapid mental shift—even tai-chi. Those didn't work.

I moved on to spirituality, new age practices, and even studied a bit of Buddhism. Again, no difference! All I felt was more exhaustion, more helplessness, more confusion. Worse, I felt like I was FIGHTING with that domineering partner all the time, thus giving her MORE attention, instead of getting her OUT of my life once and for all!

This went on for weeks and months …until one day I asked myself:

Am I not actually making things even WORSE by fighting?

What if FIGHTING, trying to find the way out, was not the answer?

What if this was not a true divorce strategy, but just a kind of avoidance?

As soon as I got this thought, I started feeling good. I finally felt like I might be onto something. So, I began a meditation and asked myself:

How can I STOP fighting, yet not stay apathetic, ignorant, or passive about it?

And then …

… I literally heard the source of my unworthiness talking directly to me, and for the very first time, saying something truly meaningful:

If you want to divorce me, you need to accept me, first—fully and unconditionally.

And that was it. That was the answer.

So, on that day, I decided to do something that seemed counterintuitive, yet it was the answer: before I went to sleep, I meditated again. As soon as I closed my eyes, the unworthiness feeling took over. But this time, I didn't fight it. I just let it be.

I acknowledged it. Embraced it. And even, in a certain way, appreciated it.

Then I said to it in my mind: "I am fully surrendering to you. Whatever it means, whatever happens next, I am giving up. I am letting go. Take me. I can't go on like this anymore. I am all yours, unconditionally." And then, I fell asleep, unaware that a day of a true hell was waiting for me.

* * *

When I woke up, I felt an indescribably strong, painful, dense feeling of ULTRA UNWORTHINESS. It felt like the very ROOT of unworthiness, the essence and "soul" of it. This sense of advanced unworthiness was exposed in its strongest, most pristine, and most hurtful state.

I felt like throwing up, but I couldn't get out of bed.

Everything felt too heavy, too painfully overwhelming. I was dizzy, in deep, internal, psychic pain, and too weak to do anything—even go to the bathroom. An endless stream of sad memories, past experiences, and stories that my mind had been creating for years popped up, confirming and magnifying the idea that "I am not worthy." My heart was literally screaming in pain.

More and more hidden layers and dimensions of unworthiness swirled up. The inner pain was indescribable. A pattern emerged over the course of that day: half an hour of long, heavy, and extremely painful unworthiness acceptance—followed by an hour of deep sleep from exhaustion, again and again, until late that night.

I have no idea how I survived that day. In some moments I felt it would be better to literally die. If I'd had any energy left, I would probably have used it to regret the *either a complete DIVORCE or one of us must die*" pronouncement I made months before—because, at that moment, I felt it was ME who had to die, instead of HER.

But I had no energy left. Sometime around midnight, I just passed out in complete exhaustion and slept the whole night like a baby.

And then, it all happened.

* * *

I still remember that morning, early in 2016. After all the previous day's "unworthiness hell," I didn't know what to expect, and I was a bit worried to open my eyes. But after the long sleep, I finally felt energized and truly rested. So, first, I checked my inner feelings: was there still some pain?

There wasn't!

In fact, I felt incredibly peaceful. Then, I carefully checked for any remnants of the feeling of unworthiness.

But these were completely gone too!

I slowly opened my eyes, walked out of the bedroom, and I noticed:

EVERYTHING FELT DIFFERENT.

My reality was filled with indescribable love. Perhaps it was true, authentic self-love. I can scarcely express what I was experiencing. I think the most accurate description is the one I gave during my Toastmasters speech on Wednesday, February 24, 2016, when I decided to openly share this experience with others. Here is some of what I said:

> *That morning, after the most painful surrendering and Letting Go I have ever experienced, I woke to the world where something was COMPLETELY different. I got out of the bed and very quickly realized that I could feel an IMMEDIATE profound connection.*
>
> ***Connection with anything and anybody in this world**—with my wife, with people around me, with strangers on the street, even with people in photos. That day, I could look at any person in the world and immediately see pure LIGHT, HOPE, JOY, and LOVE. Everything and everybody was perfect.*

I felt like a whole new life opened up to me. **I was everybody and everybody was me.** *I was absolutely connected with every-thing. I existed.*

I felt like nothing needed to be achieved, nothing needed to be deserved. It all was just there. Fulfilling. Omnipresent. Warm. And mostly— LOVING.

Everything was nothing but LOVE.

This state lasted for about eight hours, and then it disappeared.

On that day, the impossible happened:

The Unworthiness bitch was gone. Defeated, divorced, out of my life!

In her place stood the realization of the love we all already are.

The Unworthiness bitch was gone. . . . In her place stood the realization of the love we all already are.

Of course, during the following months, some rem-nants of that demon returned (like in Elton John's song "The Bitch Is Back"). Even now, she still comes to visit me, as an old friend. But she usually stays just for a few hours, or a few days maximum, and during that time I often overwhelm *her* with unconditional love, instead of regrets. And I TRULY appreciate her now. Because whenever she reappears, I learn something new, purify myself more, and then recede more deeply into the love we all already are.

But that first day, when I defeated the Unworthiness bitch, changed my life. I started valuing love more than anything else. It became my calling.

Since then, I have learned even more about unconditional love and self-love, and discovered new techniques for drawing on this amazing source of love we all already are. That is why I was privileged to literally channel this book and share the truth of ever-present love with you. So you can realize it, become it, live it, and give it too.

But how, and why, can you do this? How can you dive into this endless pool of love? Why can you share it with others?

Because you already ARE it.

Who are you truly? You are an infinite capacity of love. An infinite field of love. It's not that you are the body. Or the mind. You are the infinite capacity of infinite love first, within which lie the body and the mind. But your TRUE self is far beyond the body.

We have just been trained to identify ourselves through our bodies and our thoughts and minds, more than by the invisible field of infinite love that is here all the time. That field is still you. It is within you and you are within it. That's why unconditional love feels so great—because it is you, and you are it. You and love are inseparable. You need only to realize it.

So, let's begin.

PART I

REALIZE

The more you're willing to open your heart unconditionally, the faster you'll realize you are nothing but love. You're beautiful. You're amazing. You're powerful! You are pure love and light, looking and experiencing through the eyes of a human body.

1

WHY UNCONDITIONAL LOVE FEELS SO GREAT

Why does unconditional love feel so darn good? First of all, because it is TRUE. It is the highest of all truths.

Love is what created your entire Universe. Love is the reason you are here, your journey is here, and people in your life are here. Love emanates outward from the center of your being, your location, and those who surround you. It is a centering force.

And it is the ultimate source of your life.

Even though you might not access it all the time, it still is there, as the backdrop of your everyday being and existence, serving as the unconditional, nonjudgmental, never-ending field of energy. Unseen, it pours the very substance of life into your every movement—each word you say, each action you take, each decision you make.

Unconditional love doesn't see black or white. It just is, omnipresent and overwhelming. Yet it will never judge, never prefer or prioritize, never label, and never doubt. It is just shining perfection, expanding into infinity.

Of course, I am talking about more than *romantic* love. Yes, romance is one of the myriad possible expressions of love. But, in this book, we begin a journey to the heart of *Universal* love, the source of all things. Consider the security and comfort of knowing that you carry with you the ultimate perfection, beauty, and energy. At any time, you can draw from the source of *being*ness and *is*ness. You share with the Universe the source of expression of all forms of life. This power, if you allow yourself to use it, can become the foundation of a real-life heaven on Earth. We'll talk about this and go down that road.

But first, we must realize that the beginning of love is also the very end of the idea of SEPARATION.

Think back to when you were "in love" the last time: the feeling of loneliness vanished. It was magically replaced with an undeniable sense of inner completion. That is the true nature of universal love! In love, we realize that our feeling of being apart from others, our surroundings, and the unseen Universe, is false. That sense of separation is just an illusion.

All that previous struggle, the seemingly endless sensation of being alone and fighting this world on our own, suddenly gives way to a beautiful oneness. This new and strange state of unity conveys a feeling of COMPLETION. The world as we had known it does, at least for a moment, disappear. There remains, literally, nothing to fight. It is this sense of unity that expands our power.

It is this sense of unity that expands our power.

But, wait. This upward cycle continues.

Now, because there is nothing to resist anymore, we magically start losing all our *shields*. We open up to high states of beauty, perfection, and vulnerability, the latter an emotion that we could not previously have enjoyed. Even as we drop our shields, we paradoxically realize that we cannot be hurt anymore, as the unconditional love alone—accepting of all experiences and points of view—can never be hurt.

Our pain becomes only symbolic. This unifying, non-judgmental, perfect field of infinite love absorbs everything, including any previous idea of injustice, betrayal, and hurt. And, no surprise, once we are within love, we become un-precedentedly *forgiving!* No longer a place of mistrust and danger, the world becomes a place to be forgiven, nurtured, hugged, and healed. It becomes the recipient of the endless love that we now *must* give. Within a very short time, we exchange fighting for loving. And it feels awesome.

Why?

Because this is who we *truly* are. This is who YOU truly are.

That amazing state of miracle and abundance and shininess and conviction of the perfection of everything—including YOU—becomes a new reality. You understand that it is your REAL reality, the life that has been waiting for you behind all the perceived realities. Now, living is *easy,* and you feel at home with your new purpose, one that we all share—which is simply to be and to LOVE.

That's why unconditional love feels so great.

No more hiding.

We are—completed, worthy, fulfilled, accepted. And in this river of endless love, we start realizing we have *always* been that way, we have always been that love. We have just forgotten, and now you need to remember again.

Remember, you are nothing but L.O.V.E.

2

YOU HAVE THE POWER TO STOP PRETENDING

You probably feel that amazing potential already: the power to access the universal love within you, which is waiting to be rediscovered, reconnected to, and lived from. But here is the trick:

Love will only meet you where you are ready to meet it.

If you are holding this book, you have probably been simply AVOIDING it for most of your life. You might even fight that presumption, saying, *"That is not true! I have been looking for that source of love my entire life."* Perhaps that is why you are still seeking. Because: how can you look for something that is already HERE?

Love will only meet you where you are ready to meet it.

So, *seeking* is the wrong approach. You must first stop AVOIDING it, and then start ALLOWING it!

That is why you cannot yet access the love you already are. There is evidence of your resistance to that truth. If you weren't avoiding it, or not allowing it, you would already have been fulfilled by it. Right? We'll talk more about the feeling that love is external in Chapter 3.

Seeking unconditional love is projecting it somewhere "out there." You are literally pretending that is not within you—that you are not it. You create a limited point of view, a sort of tunnel vision based on limiting beliefs and social, cultural, and religious programming. Then, you are going through your life with experiences based on these limiting beliefs and points of view. Because the love you already are is unconditional, it lets you experience that limited point of view without any condition. Once you are exhausted by that limiting belief, you will be able to use will power and intention to drop that limiting belief and replace it with a larger and keener perspective of what you truly are.

Now, stick with me, because it gets even messier.

Because the love that is already here is UNCONDITIONAL, it means it loves you without reservation—even when you pretend it is not here and constantly push it away, or avoid it. So, it leaves you doing whatever you want (that is what "unconditional" means), including letting you feel you don't deserve it at all, or even letting you believe that love has totally abandoned you. Yet, it is here all the time, patiently waiting for you to return to it one day.

That's what I mean when I say **love will only meet you where you are ready to meet it.** If you don't want to meet it and want to keep pretending that it is not here, or that it has abandoned you, it will let you play these games. But if you decide you finally want to let go of all that nonsense, purify yourself of it, and open the door of your heart again so that it can start shining through you … then it will leap out ahead of you, but only as much as you will come before it. Not an inch more.

Of course, you might be pretending you are not pretending. Many of us have done that. It's another dimension of the game: pretending that we *are* completely fulfilled and happy, while we are not. But this is nothing more than a lie, as any pretending is. Just think: if you didn't feel the need to pretend anymore, wouldn't you feel that unconditional, fulfilling love shining through you?

Not quite. Just look around. Do you see more people being absolutely happy and living from the pure energy of love, or do you see more people PRETENDING all is fine, while simultaneously AVOIDING the truth that they are NOT?

It took me a while to figure out this seemingly obvious game of playing and pretending. Society has so elevated this ruse that many people believe the lies they keep feeding themselves every single day! That is easier than making a change.

In fact, a seemingly obvious and fundamental thing like unconditionally loving at least OURSELVES is still something most people do not even attempt. That kind of love is still very rare. I wanted to find out why. So, in late 2017, before I started writing this book, I researched the topic of love and self-love among a broad sector of people. I invested some funds in an Internet survey service called pickfu.com, to ask a total of seven hundred people questions about love and self-love. I allowed them to respond anonymously, so they would speak more freely and I could understand what was truly going on as deeply as possible.

One set of questions that I posed to fifty people was, *"Have you ever loved yourself deeply and unconditionally, at least for one day in your life? If yes, when was it?"*

Notice the word "unconditionally"—it literally means, "no condition attached." It means that you just wake up and you are deeply in love with yourself. Something as simple as that. No *if*s, *but*s, or *kind of*s … just a simple YES or NO, and WHEN (ideally, every day). I only got two or three responses like that. The rest formed a sadder story. Here are some of those answers:

> No i dont think i have ever had a day when i completely loved myself.
>
> Helpful Not Helpful · Ask Follow-Up?

> no. i often can't stand myself. I wish I could.
>
> Helpful Not Helpful · Ask Follow-Up?

> That would be a no, I have always criticized myself stemming from being criticized as a child.
>
> Helpful Not Helpful · Ask Follow-Up?

> I don't think I ever have, not for a whole day. Just a look in the mirror shows me my flaws.
>
> Helpful   Not Helpful   ·   Ask Follow-Up?

> No, I am too busy being a mother and a wife. I really wish that I could.
>
> Helpful   Not Helpful   ·   Ask Follow-Up?

So, you see that some people consider this state of mind normal. Others blame outside factors, such as how we were treated in the past, how we look in the mirror or being short on time. To the neutral observer, these are obvious excuses. While there may be some truth to them, we all have the *power* to overcome any obstacles to self-love.

But even most of those who admitted to moments of unconditional love found the need to qualify their experiences:

> Yes, it was after graduating college. From all the hard work that I had put in, I felt so proud of myself for not giving up.
>
> Helpful   Not Helpful   ·   Ask Follow-Up?

> Yes, there have been times like that when I've been extremely happy to be me. Typically this occurs on vacation. The last time was when I was in scotland.
>
> Helpful   Not Helpful   ·   Ask Follow-Up?

> Deeply and completely unconditionally probably not. But close to it, every time I feel good with myself, have the right makeup on and feel pretty.
>
> Helpful   Not Helpful   ·   Ask Follow-Up?

> After childbirth, I felt completely loved and at ease. I felt I had brought one perfect person into the world and loved myself for it.
>
> Helpful Not Helpful · Ask Follow-Up?

In so many cases, we feel the need for validation before we can indulge in self-love. That's *not* unconditional. Working hard, achieving a degree, bringing new life into the world—while still wonderful things—are all *conditions*. Loving ourselves while on vacation? Or only when we have the right makeup on? Why should self-love be relegated to few moments each year?

Then there are the people who only feel validated after having experienced pain:

> Yes, when I got a promotion at work, I worked very hard and put in a lot of overtime and effort. I was mentally and physically drained, but in the end it was worth it.
>
> Helpful Not Helpful · Ask Follow-Up?

> Yes, I have done this numerous times throughout my life. I do this and have experienced this during times of great triumph and of great despair. Each represents a high and low point where love is easier to give to oneself and make yourself wholly committed to feeling wonderful and blessed for all you have and all you are.
>
> Helpful Not Helpful · Ask Follow-Up?

> I loved myself the most on a specific day in therapy when I was told to imagine myself going about my day and doing things and ask why I am so hard on myself and beat myself up and I saw just a young woman trying her best and I realized all I could do was love myself as much as possible.
>
> Helpful Not Helpful · Ask Follow-Up?

> Yes, when my brother passed away I realized that it was time to stop worrying about the small things and start caring about things that actually matter. I could not stop greiving and I was kind to myself and realized this is part of the human condition and gave myself the care and love I need.
>
> Helpful   Not Helpful · Ask Follow-Up?

Again, sacrifice and pain are still *conditions* we require before allowing ourselves to love ourselves. Does that feel right to you? At least, acknowledging that change can happen is a first step. Here are responses from a few people who got closer:

> Yes, when I was younger I felt this way. It stopped around puberty. I still love myself fully just not unconditionally.
>
> Helpful   Not Helpful · Ask Follow-Up?

> I do this often, a few days a month.
>
> Helpful   Not Helpful · Ask Follow-Up?

> Yes. everyday I give myself a "me" time. I need it as a mom and a wife. I went out of town with my friend and enjoyed a 4-day vacation with them.
>
> Helpful   Not Helpful · Ask Follow-Up?

Do we really accept that we should only love ourselves for part of our lives? That we should love ourselves as children, or for a few days out of the month? I wouldn't call that "often," and it is certainly not the ideal, every day. Doing nice things for ourselves is, I must note, not the same as unconditionally loving ourselves, but it is also a step in the right direction. Only one person said this:

I feel I love myself everyday.

Helpful   Not Helpful   ·   Ask Follow-Up?

So, exceptions do exist, and miracles do happen.

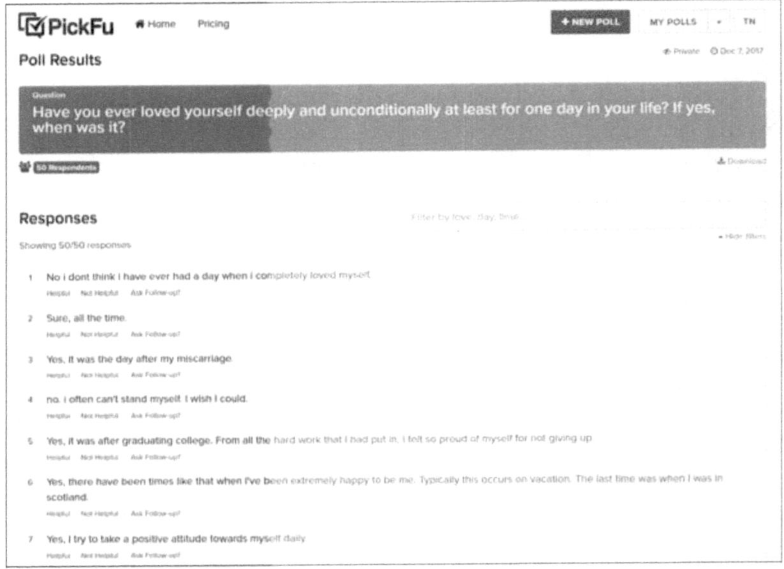

The Pickfu.com service allowed me to ask many love and self-love related questions to over seven hundred anonymous responders. I learned a lot from that, and it was one of my many inspirations for writing this book.

So, you see, the state of our society's emotional health is SERIOUS. The avoidance of love, including self-love, is common among most people.

The avoidance of the TRUTH about how we DON'T for some reason love ourselves unconditionally, may be even worse than the effects. Rather than admitting and trying to find a solution to make positive change in our lives, we cover it up and pretend that all is great with us. We only admit there's a problem when we feel completely safe, in an anonymous environment, like my untraceable Internet research. But that is about 1 percent of the time. So, 99 percent of the time, we keep lying and pretending.

I provide these examples because I want you to know you are not alone. If you can see yourself in others, you may come to understand the source and extent of your avoidance and supposed ignorance. Because, until you REALIZE and ADMIT how much you are constantly pretending, NOTHING can ever move in your life. Nothing can ever change. The love you already are will never open to you.

Let me repeat: **Love will only meet you where you are ready to meet it.**

In the space of constant avoidance, it will keep avoiding itself too.

A   B

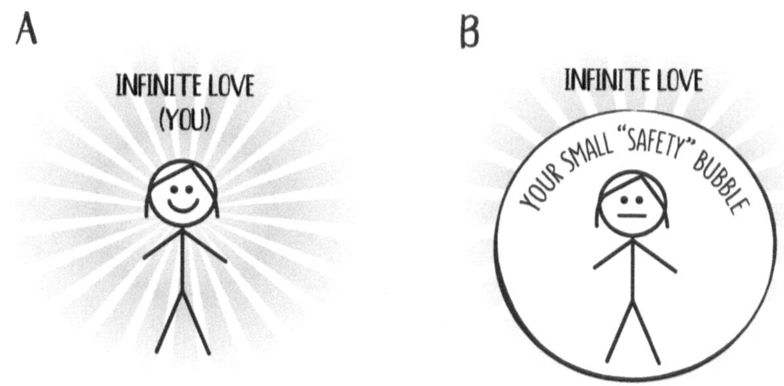

We think we are "safe" when we allow only small amounts of love to flow through our lives. We think we are "smart" by "controlling" that amount, by creating our small bubble of safety. But what are we protecting ourselves from? Simply, our own limiting beliefs. As a result, these mental bubbles keep us small and limited. There is nothing great about a "normalized and safe" life. There is nothing passionate and magic and exciting about remaining in a safe bubble. You are infinite love. That's the only place you can meet your full greatness and potential. You are infinite love, infinite power, and infinite potential. Just stop pretending you are NOT it ... and start dropping all the limiting self-beliefs. See yourself only, and only as that love.

Stop pretending. You can do it.

That's the very first step towards a pure heart, from which pure love ultimately can shine and flow.

3

IS LOVE REALLY OUT THERE?

Once you realize how much you have been pretending and start being truly honest to yourself, the doors for the love you already are will start opening up. You will stop AVOIDING. You'll enable yourself to begin ACCEPTING.

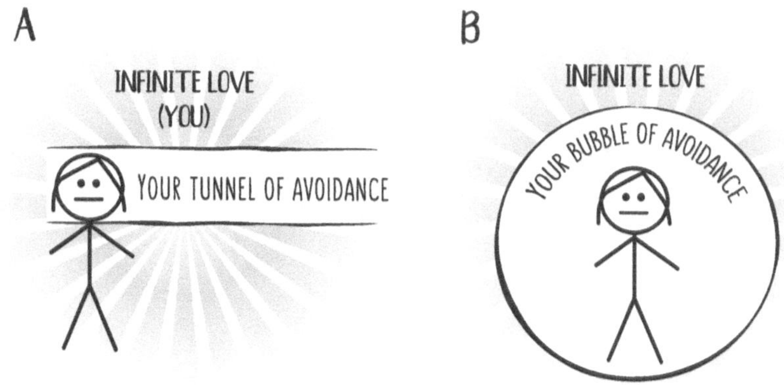

The first step to the realization of the love you truly are is tiring of the limited tunnel vision of life and the small bubble of safety you keep yourself locked in. These both are forms of avoidance. Your goal now is to penetrate through both, toward a strong desire for

27

something bigger, flowing directly from the infinite love you already are. See yourself as the highest love, because that's what you truly are.

That brutal self-honesty will start clearing out the dust in your heart and prepare you to let new, amazing things pour in. Being absolutely honest will set up a strong *intention* to finally meet the love you already are. It is like saying, "I am tired of pretending. I am tired of all that mess, the limitations, and obstacles. I am actually tired of MYSELF. I don't want to pretend anymore that all is great; I want to finally realize who I truly am."

This is a crucial step. This magical first impulse to gain a clear, honest intention will show you that a life of self-love is born in brutal self-honesty.

A brutal self-honesty will help you to start seeing your bubbles and then start popping through them. This will open your heart wider. Give yourself permission to discard all those limiting beliefs

you have about yourself. They are not true, anyway. Start believing in the unconditional love you already are. Create a strong desire to realize that love and to learn how to start living and operating from that. Fear not. Open your heart and give up your limitations.

But to stop pretending and avoiding is not enough yet. That alone, will not open the door fully. The next thing you need to realize is:

Love is NOT "out there" and never was.

All your seeking for it "out there," until now, has been pretty much pointless.

Love is not "out there" and never was.

You may still disagree, thinking, "But I have a loving husband/wife, so I DID find love out there." Well, it is not HER/HIS love you found; it is YOUR love. We will get to this in the next chapter, but before we do, let me ask you a question:

If love were TRULY somewhere out there, wouldn't the whole world live in paradise already?

If somewhere, out there in so-called external reality, lies a place called "love," what would it look like? I can guarantee you, it would be wilder than the gold rush trying to get in. There would very likely be a long queue, with millions of desperate people trying to batter down the walls to that magic place. We would probably see on the news that big companies—what we call the "heart of our economy"—would be trying to take control of that place, to make it the next must-have product for the super-rich. Politicians all over the world would surely try to take credit for it and make us believe that all that love is there only because of them.

But nothing like that is happening!

If love were really out there somewhere, wouldn't humanity have found it and begun living peaceful, loving lives? Yes. But the truth is, that's not happening. Love is NOT out there!

Not in any specific place on this planet; at least, not that I'm aware of.

And definitely not in goods, food, sex, experiences, achievements, or validation.

Nor in partners, kids, family, friends, and/or other people (we will get to that soon).

Nothing that is the true source of YOUR infinite love is separate from you. The idea that love is OUT THERE, and we must FIND IT, is a fraud. Yet, most of us act as if that were the case. We have been organizing our entire lives around this completely flawed belief.

For example, from my deep research about love and self-love, I realized that many of us put our energy into achieving the impossible, just to be finally recognized by parents or other people in our proximity and to finally feel a bit of love from *them*. Or, obsessed with our bodies and self-image, we bust our asses in gyms or hang out in clubs, trying to attract *someone* who will awaken love in us. And, many people with kids try to be good parents so they can be validated by *others* (or the kids themselves) and then feel like truly loving people.

Can you see the pattern of projecting the love we all already are to somewhere OUT THERE?

We are constantly projecting our own love "out there." And then we put conditions on that unconditional love. So, we are constantly "postponing" that love and pushing it away. There are millions of ways to do this. For example, we believe we first need to have a great body, then attract a great partner, and then experience love from him. Or that we have to be recognized first, in order to get love from parents; or be a "nice" person, to experience love from others; or be a great parent, to get love from kids in return. See how these are nothing more than internal, artificial constructs? They are artificially created stories by our minds, to keep postponing the unconditional love we already are to "sometimes in the future, when conditions X and Y are completed." Start un-believing the stories in your mind. Substitute for them a desire and intention to realize the love you already are, directly, without conditions, achievements, and self-limiting beliefs.

Yes, these all are forms of seeking love OUT THERE!

We perform these small daily actions automatically and subconsciously, and don't bother to think about WHY we do them. Everybody else seems to be doing them, so there can be nothing wrong with that. Right?

Wrong. What you are really trying to do is to OUTSOURCE the love you already ARE!

What you are doing is literally taking YOUR love that already exists WITHIN you, and projecting it OUTWARD onto to some person or object or place, and then start OUTSOURCING it from there.

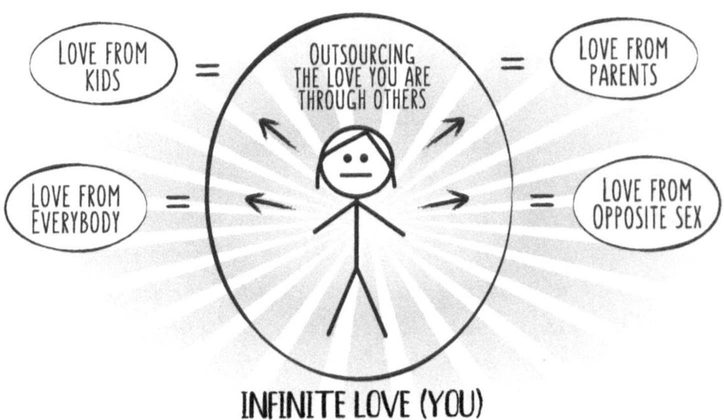

See how you are constantly trying to outsource the love you already are? You project it onto other people, places, or circumstances, and then bust your ass to get it back. But why are you projecting it out there when you already are it? Just align with it, inside yourself. Stop your projections and conditions, and ask a simple question: "If I am unconditional, infinite love already, what is my heart inspiring me to do now ... and now ... and now?"

4

WHERE IS ALL THE LOVE REALLY COMING FROM?

L et me ask you a question:

How much benefit do you receive in holding onto the belief that love is somewhere OUT THERE?

Are you happy that YOUR love is dependent on other circumstances, people, or places? Can you see how limiting this belief is, and how rare a commodity love becomes just because of it? It's time to realize that this idea is limiting, unreliable, and just plain doesn't work. If you still do persist in chasing love externally, then you don't truly love yourself.

Let me explain:

Most people think that "self-love" means loving their bodies, thoughts, opinions, hobbies, choices, preferences, intellect, memories, and other mind-produced personal content. But that's not who you truly are. That is just a bunch of attachments and egoistic labeling. What you truly are is that incredible source, potential, and capacity for love. Of course, that capacity includes your body and egoistic labels, so it is okay to love them too, as unconditional love does love everything exactly as it is. There's nothing wrong with that!

But without the full realization that YOU are love, and with the stubborn insistence on giving that power to people, things, circumstances or objects—in an attempt to outsource it back from them—you can never truly experience self-love. You must instead, realize the source of the love you already are (self) and then love and appreciate that source (love). So, self-love is about that realization first, and that never comes if you keep projecting love as OUT THERE. True self-love is about inwardness, about that source of love within you, that shines and loves unconditionally.

What is self-love? It is the realization of love as your true self. If you start building a strong conviction that you are nothing but love, this alone will start accelerating the acceptance of yourself as you are. Once you believe that you ARE love, you love yourself for that very reason. Note: You are not just your body. Your body is included in that space of love, but your true self is so much more.

In this chapter, we will do our first small, practical experiment, to show you that there is no source of love outside of YOU. To simplify things, this time I'll limit it to romantic love.

Are you ready?

Now, close your eyes and imagine the very first moment when you fell in love. If you've never been in love (that is totally okay, of course), imagine what it probably would feel like.

Tune in to the highest possible note of that love, and make it really GRAND. I want you really unleash here. Use your memories and/or imagination as much as possible and go into as many details as you can.

Remember or imagine that first kiss ... that first loving touch of hands. Recall the first moment you realized you were together in this emotion, when your heart started racing and you could not take your eyes off of one another...

How did it feel?

Focus on that feeling of BEING IN LOVE.

Remember or imagine that fully opened heart and all that love flowing out of it and into it. You were giving and taking all of what lay inside each other. Imagine the vulnerability of the moment, yet the indescribable power of being full of light at the same time.

Don't stop now. Keep that feeling flowing. Let it overwhelm you. Then, ask yourself:

Where is all that love coming from?

No, it is **NOT** coming from memories or fantasies. These are just images! It is not coming from the walls of the room you are in right now, nor from the pages of this book. Yet, if you did the exercise right and with the heart opened, here you are, overwhelmed with love. So, there must be some source. What is it? Where is it?

From **YOU**, my dear! Only from **YOU**!

You can try to deny it, not to allow it, rationalize it, or pretend it was not you. But the experience was there, and must have arisen from somewhere. Since you are alone with this book, which is an object, not the source, it could only be you.

Love always comes directly from you, because you are it.

It could only have arisen from your own space of your own presence and being.

Love **ALWAYS** comes directly from you, because you are it.

The experience of love always flows from INWARD OUT, not from OUTWARD IN. But in truth, it is not just that infinite love is within you (although the experience of it suggests that). It is that you are love, within which is the body. And the body is the vehicle through which you can experience that flow of the love you already are—of course, only if you deliberately allow it if you give yourself the permission to be that again. An intention needs to be built first, then the heart needs to be prioritized over the mind.

When you were in love for the first time, the love did not come from that person in front of you, it arose from YOU, from your own space of YOUR presence and YOUR being. And when you first saw your newly born sibling, it was again YOU within whom the experience of all that overwhelming love grew.

Now you might be asking: if all the love of the Universe is coming from within ME, how is it that I can't feel it all the time? Good question, and we will get to it. But for now, let's consider that the only reason you don't experience the love you already are more often is that you are not giving yourself PERMISSION to do so. Because you believe that unconditional love is conditional. You believe that you must meet certain requirements first, like encountering a newborn baby or a "Mr./ Ms. Perfect", to give yourself the permission to experience that unconditional love you already are. You were perfectly trained to believe that unconditional love is CONDITIONAL, dependent on external factors.

And that's all there is to this. You absorbed a story that others told.

Because I asked you to close your eyes and use your memories or imagination, you subconsciously used these instructions as another kind PERMISSION to allow yourself to have that experience. To feel that love again, without anybody or anything doing it. And of course, we were just touching the tip of the iceberg, because with more practice and mainly with deep purification (which we will talk about in the second part of this book), everything will be magnified significantly. You'll start experiencing greater blasts of love and fulfillment—without anybody doing anything, and without being in any special circumstance or location.

Love is our very nature. We are just too conditioned to allow ourselves to see it. We turned simple, unconditional love into a very complex, conditional one. But once you realize this, and you start letting go of all this conditional nonsense (or the need for these "permission slips"), the love you already are will again be allowed to shine through you unconditionally!

Remember:

Love always comes from within you only.

It always did, and it always will.

Because you already are it.

5

PERMISSION TO DITCH
THE CONDITIONS

There's no way another person can "give you love." It is simply impossible.

Whenever you "fell in love," it was not because the other person was doing something magical. Love is not something that another passes on to you in a blue Tiffany box. It is just that that person meets a finite number of requirements that you conditioned yourself to believe are necessary to the experience of unconditional love. They are permissions slips that allow the love you already are to finally show up, in a muted form.

Some people are prolific about all the conditions that need to be met to experience even a tiny bit of unconditional love. Others have so many that they make it literally impossible to ever gain that permission. This is often just a coping or defensive mechanism—a way of building a "fortress" around themselves to make it impossible for love to come into their lives while PRETENDING that they want nothing but to be loved.

We are living in an endless stream of conditions that need to be met to give ourselves permission to be the love we already are again. When we want to experience the flow of love through external outsourcing, then we set conditions like, "I first have to look like this" or "I have to achieve that." If we finally do achieve it, we only allow ourselves to let a little bit of love flow for a very short period of time. So, our desire for unconditional love is constantly faced with endless conditions. How about dropping all that conditioning, and going to the source of the love we already are directly instead? How about an unconditional ALLOWANCE? How about surrender? Wouldn't that be a faster and more direct path?

Let's get back to the fact that "falling in love" is not that somebody is GIVING you something (love). There is no magical "love spray" that the other person splashes on you, and you all of sudden HAVE love. NO!

That love already IS within you. Yes, that other person can certainly inspire you or become that permission slip to love for you, especially if that person is more aligned to the love he/she already is than you are. Other people or objects or places in our lives do have their meaning and can help us to experience the love we already are. But this doesn't happen because THEY are doing something special.

It is, again, only about YOU.

It's about YOUR intent and decision to stop outsourcing love, putting it OUT THERE, and to begin purifying yourself from all that highly conditioned behavior. It's about ending the game you have been playing all this time—pretending you are NOT love and waiting for the "right moment" or the "right person" to be it again.

Wouldn't it be more productive to ditch the conditions and give yourself FULL permission to be the love you already are, truly UNCONDITIONALLY? That means you accept love from yourself at any time, without any circumstance, object, person, place, or any other condition. What terrible thing has love done to you that makes you throw obstacles in its way? And more importantly, what is the benefit of this game? From my understanding: NONE!

So, let me repeat it:

There is no way another person can give you love.

I know it takes a big mental shift to digest this. It may take some time. And that doesn't mean you have to stop dating or having relationships or delivering babies or going to the places that represent any form of love for you! Not at all. But, if you keep seeing and looking for the source of the love you already are OUT THERE, then you can never really experience it fully. You will always be dependent on that external object, which will only limit your experience of the love you already are. This will place many more limits on your life.

Stop OUTSOURCING those permission slips, and start insourcing love.

That means, stop looking for conditions to be met to let the love from within you flow, and start giving yourself unconditional permission every single day. This takes practice, and purification of all the crap and harmful conditioning that was preventing your happiness. Little by little, you'll gain awareness and the realization that love always flows ONLY from within you, from your own space. Then you'll be able to practice living in love and giving love more than ever. Because you ARE already love.

Stop outsourcing those permission slips, and start insourcing love.

You ARE already beautiful.

You ARE already light.

You ARE absolute perfection.

You always have been it.

Be still within your heart now and feel how true that is. If you still cannot feel it, at least intuitively, then increase your conviction of it. Believe that it is there. Have some faith in yourself. For too long, you were just pretending not to be love. So, starting now, give yourself permission to be it again, *without any conditions*.

Every day, build a stronger conviction that you are nothing but love. No bubbles. No conditions. Just allowance, opened heart, and surrender.

6

A SMALL LOVE-PAUSE

The love that you already are is awaiting you. And it wants you to give it ALL the permission you can. Full, ultimate permission. No more hiding from it, no more outsourcing it, no more denying and ignoring it. And it wants you to do it NOW because NOW is the only moment you can experience it.

The love you already are is always PRESENT, and that means it is hidden in the present moment, not in the future. If you dream about meeting it sometime in the future, you are not going to meet it there; it is not present in the future, it is present in the NOW. That's why many people wait for love too long; because they are constantly *postponing* it to the future, instead of starting to access it now.

Along with thoughts about meeting it in the FUTURE, trying to "understand" it instead of directly experiencing it, will postpone it until "NEVER." So, you can experience it NOW, or you can be thinking about it instead of realizing it.

The love you already are lives in presence, in the NOW, and doesn't align with your postponement-based thoughts. In fact, it doesn't care about any thoughts, it only cares about your heart.

It wants you to open it more and more, so the present moment can be experienced through that, thus it has a portal through which to start flowing.

Have you ever noticed that presence can only be lived and felt, but never thought? This is what being in the moment is all about. How many thoughts have you ever needed in a perfect present moment, during which nothing but love was flowing? And how many times has that state been interrupted when thoughts break in?

You see, thoughts do not direct you into the present moment and, thus to the source of the love you already are. Mind is too overrated. True power comes from heart.

Mind is too overrated. True power comes from heart.

So, to open the source of the love we already are, we do not actually need to achieve or do something. What we need to do is the opposite—to let go of as much as possible, including your conditioned beliefs and behaviors related to unconditional love and your effort to "think" love and "think" the present moment. Don't worry; you will discover how to bypass those obstacles in the next part of this book.

But before that, I want to use this small love-pause to give you a glimmer of what is to come:

Pause all your thoughts for a few seconds right now and feel only the present moment.

The emptiness of it.

The non-conditions, non-neediness arising from it.

The peace of it.

Yes, that is the perfect environment from which love grows—and if you've felt it before, that's where it came from. Unconditional love does not need any conditions, mind, or thoughts. It only needs your mind-free presence, with your heart being opened. We were falsely trained to believe that we first need to achieve, sacrifice, be perfect, obey, follow, make others happy, or do thousands of other (often unachievable) things to experience love, or at least start welcoming it in our lives.

In doing those things, we were not living in the true presence of love. We were only living in "when-land" and "perhaps-one-day-land." In the false belief that "only when this happens, and that condition is met, will I achieve that or this. Then, love, joy, fulfillment, and happiness will, PERHAPS, flow," (at least for a few seconds. So I'll bust my ass for months and years to experience that few seconds of unconditional love sometime, later on.)

Can you now see how we are constantly *postponing* being who we truly are until it becomes a habit that we even stop questioning? How we are postponing love, because we believe it is not only OUT THERE in objects, but also out there in TIME?

So, pause for a small moment now, take a deep breath, exhale, empty your mind—and admit, that for too long, you have been living in a future-land.

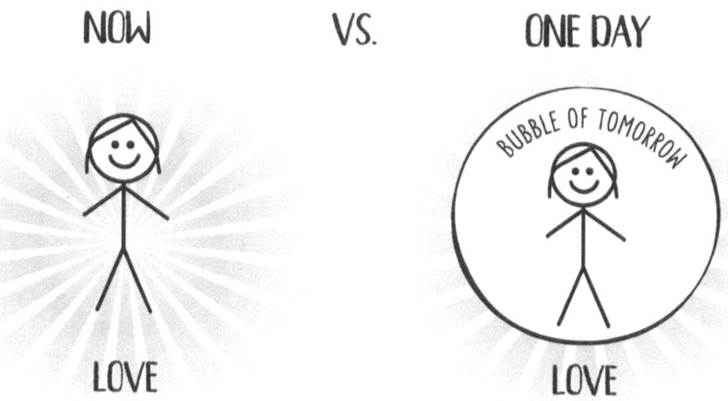

Being in the love NOW, versus being in the bubble of tomorrow-land. Notice that both are only now, anyway: Love as well as the bubble. But as long as you remain attached to the bubble of "tomorrow," this bubble with you in any other "now," you will stay in that bubble in any other "now." Thus, that desired "tomorrow" will never come. Your NOW bubble represents all the NOWs. So, you need to choose in every NOW moment what you truly prefer. Do you prefer to stay living in the bubble of tomorrow? Or do you prefer the actual love you already are? Choose your preference, and then bring it to NOW. Experience it as if it already is the truth. Insist on that preference now, and now, and now... and any other now.

And then ... bring that future into NOW.

Again, imagine that ALL your conditions for experiencing the deepest love of this Universe are met. Don't rationalize, don't think too much, just imagine it. Whatever it is.

There is nothing outside of now. Even your projection of the ideal and desired future is happening now. But if you keep this projection in every subsequent now, in all "nows," all you will keep experiencing is this projection and "hope" of tomorrow. Thus, detach from the projection and go for the desired results. What do you want from all your effort and all your stories in the future? Feel into it NOW. Bring that feeling of the end result into NOW. And start living it NOW. Give yourself full permission to live the energy, feeling, and vibration of your ideal future NOW. Otherwise, you will be locked in your bubble of the "future-land" forever. There is only now. Whatever you want to experience, you need to bring it to now. Thus, start living the experience and feeling of unconditional love you already are NOW.

Imagine your perfect partner, perfect house, your kids living a beautiful, peaceful life, the entire planet living in peace, politicians not being politicians anymore but just pure love (I know this requires a lot of imagination, but at least try), kids in Africa not starving anymore.

Imagine anything it takes to have ALL your conditions, to give yourself the ultimate, full permission to FEEL overwhelming love, to tell yourself "all is good now, and I finally can rest and feel peace and love"—that love you have been postponing into the future for so long.

Just do it, whatever effort it takes.

Keep working on that, until you bring that state of love BEINGNESS from the very distant future, to NOW. Tell yourself: "I feel the love now and I AM that love now." Got it?

Congratulations, you are finally moving somewhere! For just this moment, you are finally living the love you already are in the PRESENT, instead of putting it off. Because you already ARE it now.

It is already here.

NOW.

And NOW.

And NOW.

And NOW.

And NOW.

And NOW.

Just open your heart and be it. You don't need to change yourself at all to experience it! You only need to change your belief from "it is OUT THERE" and "OUT IN THE FUTURE," to "IT IS ALREADY HERE, RIGHT NOW."

It only takes a bit of practice. Are you finally realizing it? Bravo!

Even thinking about something happening "tomorrow" instead of feeling the end result NOW is nothing more than giving your power away again and then outsourcing it. The "tomorrow" is another out-there, another limitation, another indirect path, another postponement. You see, we can use not only people and circumstances as postponements and excuses but also time—specifically, the future. So, break the limiting tunnel vision of "tomorrow", and start feeling your way toward the desired outcomes NOW. Start experiencing and living them NOW. Because the unconditional love you already are is here NOW. And NOW. And NOW. And NOW. Break through your bubbles and excuses, and start tuning into it NOW.

7

YOU ARE AN EXTRAORDINARY POTENTIAL OF LOVE

You are holding this book because it called you. It called you because of your strong inner desire to awaken to the deepest love you already are. Radiate that love, and start making a real difference in this world.

You represent an extraordinary potential.

You are a diamond that needs to be shaped and polished to shine its pristine perfection, sourced from YOU—the very source of unconditional love.

It doesn't matter how you label your physical expression (body), your past experiences, or your current life situation, or the way the endlessly ignorant society labels you. In other words, it doesn't matter what your minds thinks and projects about your current state of being and living. All of those things are artificial, mind-based constructions.

Because, in reality, you already are love, and that is the only truth.

Everything else is here for you, and FROM you, to help you navigate toward that source of the love you already are, so you can become a purer and more beautiful, magical expression of that love. You just need to WANT to start seeing that, you need to have a true, honest, authentic DESIRE to finally be it again. Not to get more out of this life, or to acquire more social validation, but just the opposite. Start GIVING to the world, because now you finally can. Release the strictures of obsolete social conditioning, dogmas, past experiences, cultural biases, or religious beliefs.

None of that matters in the light of the love you already are, especially once you start shining it again. Sure, you can have fun and continue living your life as you please; everything is allowed here by unconditional love! But all these are ADDITIONS to your very nature—the pristine, perfect, miraculous love you already are.

So, I encourage you, start shifting your focus, start thinking AS love, and you realize more and more how your physical life expression is here to serve love, to give love, and to change the whole energy and vibration of this collective human consciousness. Stop thinking about what you can take from this life. Instead, get back to the love you already are, and start giving and creating from that. You will become, again, the true, miraculous love creator.

Be that love, radiate that love through your beingness, and you will realize a whole new reality and life with it. If you are reading this book, you are a man or woman with extraordinary potential to GIVE love. You will realize that potential through your most natural love-vibrations, those that come from within you, from the deepest place in your heart, not from your body.

Yes, realizing that potential will require some courage, desire, and deliberateness, which may be difficult in today's socially conditioned world. It will require some heavy lifting, too, which we will start doing in the next part of this book. But it is your true privilege and your duty to do so—for both yourself and others.

Just increase that courage, desire, and deliberateness. Insist on nothing but becoming a purer and purer expression of the perfect love you already are. I already see you that way; I already see that potential in you. And all I am is another reflection of your own consciousness. So, in fact, it is YOU talking to YOU, saying that you CAN have the ultimate faith in yourself, you CAN give yourself that realization of that ultimate perfection you already are. You are an extraordinary being.

I already see you that way; I already see that potential in you.

You are an extraordinary potential love.

The whole planet can change just because of YOU. Your past actions or experiences do not matter anymore. Forget them. Forgive them. Forgive yourself.

Anything that happened to you until now, happened to help you realize that you are NOT any nonsense. You are NOT what others might have been telling you. You are NOT your past decisions or actions.

You are perfection.

A perfect, beautiful love.

Wake up.

Realize it, and make the ultimate decision to become it permanently. To be nothing BUT it. It's time to awaken. Others are already doing it. Do not stay behind! There's no benefit in postponing the realization of the extraordinary potential you are.

I already love you unconditionally. And that means YOU already love YOURSELF unconditionally. Because these words are a reflection of you. You have brought this book to your reality to realize that reflection, to realize you do not need anything (including this book or me) to love yourself unconditionally.

So, do it.

Give yourself a huge hug and caress. Right now. Because you're just awesome.

PART I: Questions & Answers

Q: If I understand this properly, the whole idea behind this concept is that I am the source of all the experiences, because the experience is always coming directly from me. Is that right?

First of all, this is not a CONCEPT but a REALIZATION. Conceptualization is a mind-made description, which is nothing but a certain combination of words, to which we give meaning in the language we are used to thinking in. So, there is not really any direct realization in conceptualization. If we want to REALIZE love, we have to move away from THINKING love.

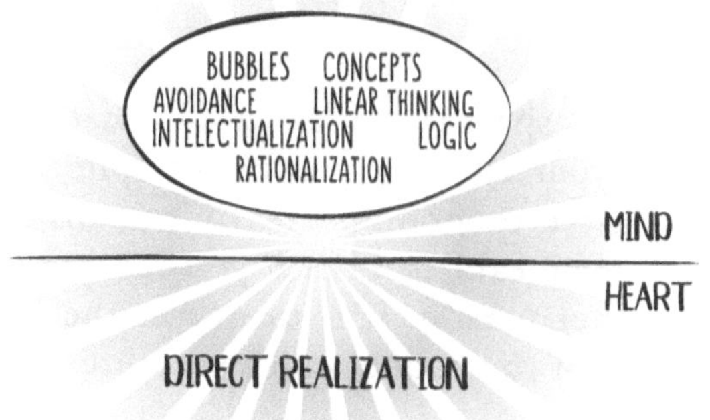

Mind will always only create more concepts, bubbles, rationalizations, and other distractions to keep you from heart. Those will never help you realize the love you already are. You cannot think your way toward the love you already are. You can only experience it from heart. That's the only place the direct realization can come from. Thus, you need to start prioritizing your heart and start opening it more and more. Your infinite heart is far more powerful than your mind, which is full of limiting artificial beliefs.

That's why I specifically asked you at the very beginning of this book to read it with an opened heart first. It doesn't matter much how you reassemble the text from this book in your mind to make a concept out of it, to give yourself an impression you "understand." Conceptualization will not get you closer to an actual realization, thus it is not important how you "understand" this book. It is rather about how you "feel" this book, or more precisely, what realizations you have while reading it. The goal of this book is not having a more intellectual understanding, as it is with most similar books. The goal is to open your heart as much as possible and start feeling that love you already are DIRECTLY.

Q: What is the practical aspect of the realization of the love we already are? For example, how does that help me when I date a man?

The most practical aspect is the realization that you don't *need* anything outside yourself to fill the void (despite years of social, cultural, and religious programming). That means that realizing you are love is not meant to HELP you reach a goal, or find union with another person. It is to *become* the ULTIMATE GOAL, from which you should make your life choices.

So, if you are looking just for a tool to "help you" when you date a man, you are still acting from a lack of belief, or that the love you already are is OUT THERE. You are still giving all the love power to an external object. For example, when you go on a date, you start out with EXPECTATIONS. You expect something to happen, based on the artificially constructed set of demands you think must be met to give yourself the permission to feel love. Usually, the less you truly want to experience love, the more complex this set of "wants" and "must-be*s*" is. The guy you are dating seems too "needy," too "fancy," "doesn't really know what he wants," etc. When, instead, you truly "let go" of all that, you are ready to accept love. (We will talk in depth about letting go in the next part of this book.)

Now, imagine you go on the same date, but with ALL THE EXPECTATIONS MET before it even happens. You already ARE in love; it is within you. So you don't really go on a date to get something from it, because there is nothing to get. In fact, you now even think about how to GIVE something to it, how to contribute something to it, because you are a pristine love already.

Q: It all makes sense, and I have been already feeling it intuitively for a long time. Yet, the practice of it in "real life" seems to be somehow challenging.

There are usually several reasons why it seems to be that way. First, the belief itself that there is something called "real life" besides the love you already are, and that "it is challenging," comes from long-term social programming.

In general, we have been accepting the wrong human ideas that love is external and that we must achieve for it, fight for it, look a certain way for it, behave a certain way to get it. So, now, we subconsciously believe that unconditional love cannot flow if we don't perfectly adapt to our social environment, and are not accepted by the entire social matrix first.

So, most of the time, we prioritize social adaptation and social validation instead of BEING LOVE.

Do you really think that meeting all the social conditions in order to gain permission to feel love actually works? Judging by the endless stream of conditions that continues when you meet the first requirements, I'd say no.

If living from the love you already are seems to be still too challenging, it is likely a case of mistaken priorities—of putting social validation first. This only postpones your realization of the love you already are.

My advice? Screw social rules, social dogmas, the social matrix. Prioritize love and love only. Live it. Be it. And then start acting and creating FROM it, instead of BECAUSE OF IT, or even worse, FOR IT.

Become a true love-rebel. You can be the one to help society wake up. You don't need social validation and social approval to be love and loved. You already are love.

Q: *Can you better explain what you mean by "outsourcing love"?*

The conventional way we were trained to think of love, thanks to culture, books, fairy tales, Hollywood movies, etc., includes a "middle man" (or woman, baby, someone, some time, or something ELSE). This THIRD entity gets between us and love—the two real parts of the equation.

It goes like this:

First, you create the idea you are not love and that you are separate from it. You create that "bubble" of separation from the love you already are. And then you start seeing yourself as somebody who needs to find love, fight for love, etc. Your reality will start supporting that belief out of the unconditional love you already are, which supports you in any experience and belief you want to have, including the highly limiting and untrue beliefs.

Second, all these limiting beliefs and ideas of separation, enforced by general social, cultural, and religious beliefs, will start making you believe more and more that love is *OUT THERE* (your artificially created tunnel vision), so you project it to someone or something else (plus into the future).

And on top of that, you also skillfully create a lot of personal conditions and ideas about what that love should be and feel like, what it should look like. And you become very stubborn about those ideas, conditions, limiting beliefs, and limiting self-stories. Of course, all this will create the never-ending maze of seeking and frustration—all based on limiting (self)beliefs and the idea of separation from the love you already are. But what would your life look like without all those limiting (self)beliefs? What would your life be like without the deeply rooted conviction that love is somewhere out there, that it is something externalized, that you need to "prove" yourself for first? What would your entire reality look like if you believe and know and FEEL every second that you are nothing but love and perfection already? It is entirely up to you which beliefs you want to build your life around.

How much more love could you experience without the interference of endless conditions and permission slips? What if you ALLOW the love to be here all the time and didn't try to outsource it first? What if you give YOURSELF permission to be the only permission slip? And then make the deliberate choice to open your heart fully and start living FROM the love you already are, despite what anybody thinks or says? Bring some love and kindness and warmness to this world by being what you truly are: L.O.V.E.

The world of permission slips and conditions and outsourcing is too limiting. What if your one million conditions are met for a certain period of time (a seemingly perfect partner, for example) and then a lot of them happen to go "un-met"? Then you will stop giving yourself permission to keep being the love you already are, and you will become more and more addicted to the external permission slips and to the process of outsourcing. Thus, you'll be locked in the vicious circle of seeking and more (self)limiting beliefs. But what if you start becoming addicted to the love you already ARE instead, and then start living, meeting people, creating, being, and giving out of that? Your choice!

The direct path is to surrender all your conditions, ideas, stories, permission slips, tunnel visions, validation addictions (which are also forms of permission slips to feel love), and personal bubbles, so that you can merge with that field of the love you already are again, directly. Thus, stop outsourcing, and instead align to your higher self, without any separation. How? We will talk about this in the second part of the book.

Wouldn't it be better to stop OUTSOURCING love and start BEING THE SOURCE of love?

Here is the difference between "outsourcing" and the direct experience:

Now, the direct realization is a new space from which you can finally start creating and living an idea not focused on your lack of anything. You already have it all. That's the only place from which magic and miracles can come back into your life.

PART II

THE 'YOU ARE LOVE' PROCESS

Love is simple. Love is omnipresent.
Love is always already here.

But it has been covered up with too much of a noise.
Too much of "crap of life".
Too much of painful past experiences.
Too much of nonsense.

The 'You Are Love' process is here to get you back to that
simplicity and higher truth of love.
Back to the love you already are.

With its simple, powerful 3-steps,
you'll be back in love in no time.

8

IF IT'S NOT LOVE,
IT'S NOT YOU

Let me ask you a simple question:

When somebody tells you that you are not good enough, how does it feel?

It pretty much sucks. Right? Of course, it does. Because it is not true!

First of all, you can never be "not good enough". You can play such a game with yourself (pretending not being enough), but you can do it only because you *are* good enough to even play such silly games with yourself!

In the field of the unconditional love you already are, you are allowed to play any games with yourself, and you will be supported in them unconditionally. The very basis of your existence, the love you already are, will never place any conditions on you wanting to express yourself, including self-destructive expressions, like believing you are not worthy.

But that doesn't mean that the love you already are will keep looking at you without any responses. That love you already are wants you to shine as much as possible because all it knows and all that matters to it is love. So with any action or thought, it will certainly produce emotional feedback. If that feedback is painful and negative, then it is literally telling you, "This is NOT true!" If you are willing and able to listen to the subtlest vibrations of your heart, you will realize it is not true too.

What you might not know now is that *how you interpret* that feeling coming from the love you already are is up to you. And we were trained to interpret everything through brain first, instead of through heart.

We were trained to interpret everything through brain first, instead of through heart.

Consider that how others perceive you is based on highly biased personal opinions and projections. So, if you hear this highly personal unworthiness projection from a person we were trained to believe we should "respect and listen to," you THINK he or she is right. You start believing you are NOT worthy, and you don't care that your whole body and heart are screaming, "Stop, this is not true!" Trained to suppress our feelings and not to listen to them, and socialized to prioritize the brain, mind, science, and logic over the heart and love, we simply don't listen to our hearts anymore. We can change that!

Now, let's look at another example:

How do you feel if somebody says, "You are a beautiful being, you are shining with so much kindness. I so much love your opened heart. I truly appreciate you, and I love you."?

You feel GREAT. Right? Of course, you do—unless you enjoy playing the game called "not allowing" or "forever not enough."

Then, you do all in your power to make this statement NOT be true. Yet, you still feel something good and warm deeply in yourself, despite all the denial.

Because it is TRUE! Your heart does intuitively know that already—that you are nothing but love, completely made of love!

But here is the trick again:

Because we were skillfully "trained" and manipulated into believing what others are saying about us is MORE IMPORTANT than what we feel and how deeply we are connected with our own hearts and the love we already are, we started:

1) believing that any observation others make about us is inherently true; and

2) becoming VALIDATION ADDICTS.

Let me tell you more about these two things because once you understand them fully, it will be much easier for you to start practicing the purification techniques I am about to share in this part of the book. After exposing all the lies you have been unhappily living with, the intent to become once more the pure love you already are will magnify tremendously.

BELIEVING THAT OBSERVATIONS ABOUT YOU ARE INHERENTLY TRUE

When you were born, you were nothing but love. That's why you were attracting so much care and love because you were shining, nothing but perfection.

But as you started growing, people around you decided not to see perfection in you anymore. Most are not able to see it in themselves, so they project the same on others. Then, they started pushing you to conform with the same social, cultural, and religious norms and standards they were pushed toward (mostly without even questioning them). And they started by comparing you to what they know as "norms" (there are not any norms; that's just a stupid social construct) and noting any "deviations" they found in you.

For example, I have a friend who has a four-year-old boy. He's a great kid, who spends a lot of time in his own world. That's what kids do. Some kids share this space with others; some don't.

This child shares less than many, but because the larger group of kids are outgoing and very social, and do share their worlds, his mother decided he doesn't fit the "norm" she created in her mind. She started calling him a "shy boy." Whenever somebody asks him a question and he doesn't reply, his mother immediately "apologizes" for him, saying, "He is just shy."

This is a personal opinion based on the need to constantly keep comparing others to the "average" created by that personal observation. This label was forced on the boy so often that he started saying the same thing: "I am shy."

So, he was made to believe a personal opinion based on comparison with a fabricated "norm," which he thought was an "observation of truth." Thus, the young boy was given an attachment of "shyness"—all because he was told that adults are always right, and he needs to listen to his parents (as if we adults are always more clever than kids).

So, the perfect love this boy already was got obscured by an attachment called "shyness." (He didn't even pick this attachment deliberately; it was just superimposed onto him.)

Now, I am not judging the people in this example—not at all! No one is really at fault, as we all are trained to think and believe similarly. The majority of people: a) lack awareness; b) are not aligned to the love they already are; and c) don't believe they can be anything else, and surely not perfection and pure love, because for most of their lives they have not been validated in this way *by others*. They believe that they are what others think about them.

So we are blindly taking highly personal opinions (mostly distorted by inner insecurities and misalignment from the heart of the one who is expressing these opinions) as "truths," and we are building an endless number of attachments around the love we already are, until we completely cover it up and start living from these false attachments. We treat them as truth, rather than the amazing source of love we already are.

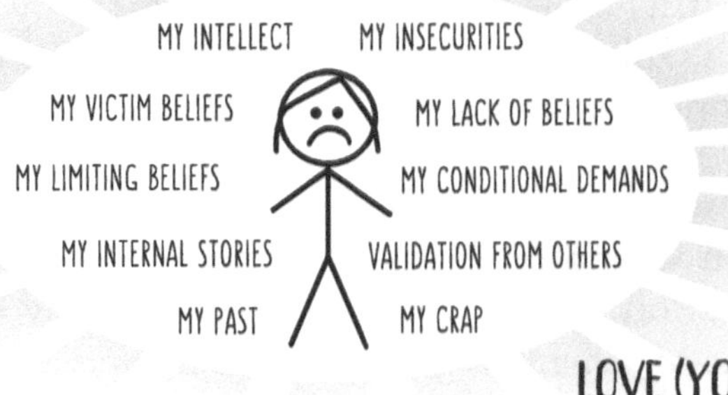

Too many attachments hide the love you already are. All these attachments create one huge bubble. You are not your crap! Nor your internal stories. Nor your intellect. Nor your past. Nor your not-good-enough beliefs.... You are love. Pure, pristine love. The sooner you start letting go of your attachments, the more quickly you will realize this directly.

Even worse, we start calling these attachments "personality" and "characteristics"—but that's just because nobody has been telling us repeatedly, "Your only true characteristic and personality is the love you already are—everything else is an unnecessary addition."

It's no surprise that so many people on this planet suffer, from a young age. They may be constantly forced to play false roles that they have not chosen (like "being shy") and don't know where they are truly coming from and or the true source of their being!

You are NOT what others say.

You are NOT your education.

You are NOT your opinions.

You are NOT your preferences.

You are NOT your style.

You are NOT your hobbies.

You are NOT your achievements.

These all are still just ATTACHMENTS.

But, in the center of all of them, or in the background, if you like, lies your TRUE self: LOVE. You've just created too many attachments and placed them OVER that centeredness—over the love you are. So, your heart was buried beneath the mind and its mind-created attachments.

Because of this skillful "social training," you have very little space to shine the love you already are, and you require that third party to "allow" you to love. You have come to rely on that, so you can avoid and postpone your own love realization. Let's look at how to overcome that.

LIVING AS A VALIDATION ADDICT

Not only were you trained to accept others' perceptions of you as true, over time but you also became highly ADDICTED to that belief! It affects your thoughts and actions. You became a true validation addict.

Acquiescing to this pointless social game makes you constantly ask yourself:

Who am I in the eyes of others?

Once you start believing that the distorted personal opinions of others are true (as if the opinion of another would ever matter to what IS), you start being obsessed by manipulating others to have as many "positive" personal, totally irrelevant thoughts about you as possible. You crave that. And you're not alone. For 99 percent of people, this is not only subconscious and automatic but also literally inevitable. Addiction is difficult to end, but it can be done.

YOUR VALIDATION ADDICTIONS

What is the true source of your well-being and self-love? The love you already are, or the positive validation from others? How much you are addicted to these things? How well have they been working for you so far? How much self-doubt have they created, compared to moments of true well-being and the flow of authentic, unconditional (self) love? Break free from the validation addiction, and your well-being and self-love will be elevated instantly. Love doesn't need any validation. It just is, and it shines effortlessly. There are no insecurities in the presence and beingness of love. Thus, no validation addiction is needed—as its only purpose is to compensate for your insecurities and limiting (self)beliefs.

Here is how you become a "validation addict." First, you start manipulating yourself, by fitting your appearance, behavior, thoughts, opinions, and daily actions into what you think will look good in the eyes of OTHERS, so you can get positively validated and then give yourself permission to feel "good." You probably won't admit this, because part of the common social protocol in many cultures can be hiding your feelings, especially good ones, from others. By doing this, you not only trade the love you already are for validation, but you build your life around the flow of neediness (for positive validation) instead of the flow of pristine love you already are. You start pretending you are something you're NOT.

You are not how other people see you. Their view is always distorted, subjective, and biased by their own insecurities and projections. Stop trying. Stop being a validation addict. You are love. See only that. See yourself only as that. Put your effort into shining that love and living from that (without expecting any form of validation as a "confirmation" that you "really" are it from others). Shine it unconditionally. Brighten up your whole reality with that. Vibrate from your highest frequency of love. And see what happens. Without expectations and the neediness to be validated for it, or getting any kind of "confirmation" of it. What you truly believe in doesn't need any confirmation. And the confirmation from other people is very rarely honest and pure.

And because there is ALWAYS somebody that the mostly ignorant and blind "OTHERS" will compare you to, you are in a trap without an end, forever.

You can never be enough in the eyes of others. NEVER. One day they will you call "weak", so you will work hard to become the president of the United States. As soon as this happens, they will call you "arrogant and not humble enough." You will ALWAYS be compared, ALWAYS be judged. There is no end to it.

That's the whole idea of this social matrix: to set the rules so that you can never truly feel you are enough. So you can be manipulated. You need to keep consuming to fill that void with more products, more validation, more food. You can stay a sheep in the world, in which 5 percent of people control 95 percent of EVERYTHING on this planet, while literally sucking all the love out of it.

You keep plugging into this matrix until you make the very deliberate decision to "unplug" from this nonsense and try a different way, as I did years ago. Because nobody can take from you the love you already are. You are the only one who can take it from yourself—by remaining hypnotized by the social conditioning and manipulation you have been subject to all your life.

You need to reclaim that love you already are.

You are love.

A beautiful perfection.

And it is NOT your fault that you have been coerced into believing something else. We all were manipulated into this bizarre social straitjacket and became bound by it. That's why you are holding this book. We all want to be free of it again. We want to stop playing games to "look good in the eyes of others." We all want to get rid of this nonsense and let the love flow again.

We want to stop pretending.

That's why we need to fully realize the source of our own love, the love we already are. Then we can connect to it and live from THIS—rather than from social validation. The real source of your well-being can only be the love you already are. Because if it is not love, it is not you.

9

THE LOVE SEEKER'S DEATH

When you feel truly connected, when you feel love flowing, when you feel your heart being opened fully—does your education matter? Does what you are wearing matter? Does what car you drive matter? Does if you are "shy" or "eccentric" matter?

NO!

And when you feel nurtured and connected and loved, how much does it matter whether you label yourself "feminist" or "pacifist" or "democrat" or "intellectual" or "artist" or "vegan"?

If your heart is pumping from love and you are in the flow of amazing magic, those things don't matter! That's because you are NOT all these attachments. You are love, and the more you are opened to only THIS, without all the unnecessary additions, everything is perfect!

See that paradox: you have been acquiring all these additions and labels and attachments all your life—to feel acknowledged and appreciated and admired—but you truly feel the best, at your absolute highest, during the simplest moments when you need

NONE of them! The love you already are will ALWAYS feel better than all the attachments in this world combined. That's also why you must learn to let go of all these attachments. If you let them go in your mind, then you don't give them any more significance, and their effect on you will disappear.

So, these attachments covering the love you already are will stop clouding your consciousness, and you will start shining love and perfection again. And this world needs love! This planet needs you to shine it as much as possible!

So, please, understand, that love is not about seeking. Nor it is about acquiring things, knowledge, validation, likes, friends, or achievements. That is all just diversion, a dead end, postponement, and a sure source of misery. Becoming the love you already are is about the very opposite of seeking and acquiring:

It is about LETTING GO of who you are NOT.

Once you let go of all the distractions we all are full of, perfection will be free to arise again. Without the attachments of who you are not, you reveal the truly pure, beautiful, connected, authentic, and innocent person you really are again. It will feel like the moment when you were in love for the very first time. You will feel fully at ease, full of peace, love, and appreciation. Everyone will want to connect with you—but take care that you don't see this as another avenue toward social validation. And that's what this second part of this book is about:

Letting fully go of who you are NOT.

Letting go of your crap ... of your overfilled mind ... of your maze of confusing emotions.

It will be challenging sometimes, but you will survive this. I did. And I know that, at the end of it, you will come out purer than ever. You'll be free to shine more and more with love every single day.

Your job? Let go. Let the love-seeker die.

You cannot find "out there" what is not there. The focus on seeking will keep you in the loop of seeking. The focus on the love you already are will get you closer to that state every single day until you become it once again.

Your job? Let go. Let the love-seeker die.

It is as simple as that.

Let all the ideas of the need to achieve, compare self with others, deserve, be seen, or be positively validated by others in order to give ourselves a small permission to feel a bit of love, die.

Just imagine your life without all this hassle. Wouldn't THIS give you a whole new energy and purpose to live, create, inspire, give, and possibly transform the lives of many other people? Living from the confidence of love you already ARE is a whole new life experience. Or, would you really prefer staying a validation addict instead? Giving your power away and outsourcing your well-being for the few brief moments when somebody validates your image?

Do you really want to have the same life as everybody else, based on social norms, compliance, and conformity? Do you want to keep listening to their "truths" about "one cannot live from love alone" and "this is not reality"? That is THEIR reality, THEIR limitation, THEIR misery.

In other words, do you want to remain a love-seeker, begging others for the love you already ARE?

I know you don't. That's why we need this realization, to start deliberately waking up. Are you afraid that you might stand out? That love will overwhelm you? So, what?

Stand out! Inspire! Be rebellious!

All you have to do is let the love-seeker die. If you are holding this book, you are more than ready to do it. Stop all the excuses. Stop postponing. Do not pretend anymore. To get back to your pristine love state, realize that you are already in it. You always have been. Now you must willingly return to your ultimate, beautiful perfection. Radiate. Then radiate some more.

Make this place a heaven. And help to heal this planet with the power of love. Proclaim: "The love-seeker is dead! Long live the only true source of love!"

10

STEP #1: LETTING GO

Now, let's start doing some actual purification work.

The very first step of the 'You Are Love' process I am going to share with you is called "Letting Go." And it is the method behind my "Unworthiness bitch" breakthrough, which I shared with you in the introduction.

Do you still remember how everything with my fight with unworthiness started changing? It was when I said to myself: *"I am fully surrendering to you. Whatever it means, whatever happens next, I am giving up. I am letting go. Take me. I can't go on like this anymore. I am all yours, unconditionally."*

Remember how I experienced my encounter with the love we all already are for the very first time? The *letting go* was the biggest part of it. Let me tell you more about that now.

When I was going through my battle with the Unworthiness bitch, I was seeking help in many books as well, one of which made a huge difference. It's called, *Letting Go: The Pathway of Surrender*, by David R. Hawkins. I felt a definite synchronicity with this book, and, despite its four hundred pages, I finished it overnight.

What I read made surrendering and letting go make sense to me for the very first time, and I knew I was meant to move toward that. Although the book covered some amazing perspectives on how "letting go" can totally change your life in the most positive way, it didn't tell me how to do that. But my desire to let go was very deep. I felt I was too full of the crap I had gathered from past experiences, struggles, disappointments, heavy social conditioning, and all kinds of unhealthy attachments. I knew it was time to let go of most of it—starting with the Unworthiness bitch.

So, I spent months trying to figure it all out. I used meditations and tried different experiments to discover the easiest way to release our internal crap. I spent long hours in "letting go" mode, observing myself and the immediate effects, to see what worked and what did not. The progress was slow, yet there was some every day. Intuition, faith, stubbornness, and a high level of awareness helped a lot. After some time, I finally was able to isolate a few exact steps that more often than not led to results. Anything that provided immediate relief and the sensation of letting go of internally stored crap was a positive step. The climax of that effort was, as you already know, my very first meeting with the love we all already are. And it was MIND BLOWING.

So, that's how the Letting-Go Process became my first tool for cleaning out the crap all of us carry around. Since **There is always something to let go of, to detach from.** then, I use it often. I have made it a habit, to replace the habit of clinging to attachments. There is always something to let go of, to detach from. Once you get into it, you really start enjoying it and even crave it—the emptiness, lightness, peacefulness, and fulfillment coming from letting go and surrendering. Once you taste it, you'll want more!

That's why I didn't want to keep the letting-go process to myself. So, I started sharing it with other people. I shared it at first with friends, who acknowledged immediate results, and then later—with the help of my friend Maria—with the general public.

Maria is an amazing woman with a truly opened heart. She understood the impact this information could have, so we started improving the Letting-Go Process together, to make it easily understandable to anyone. After a few months, we decided to put the whole system on a website for free. We called this project www.LettingGoMovement.com. The web page is still live; you can check it out yourself.

I'll share with you here some of the great feedback we got, so you'll know what to expect before you move on to the technique itself:

Source: www.LettingGoMovement.com

So, again, the process works and has been fully tested and proven. A lot of credit goes to my friend Maria too!

Source: www.LettingGoMovement.com

A Word Of Inspiration And Gratitude From "LET GO!" Technique Founders...

The Letting Go Movement, which we have established together with Maria and our mutual friend Jan, shared the powerful Letting-Go Process with many other people. (In the picture, Maria, the co-founder of the Letting Go Movement, is on the left.)

Know this: you are not your crap. You have been traumatized by this life for too long already. It is time to let go.

Let go of what?

EVERYTHING that is not love.

Everything that clouds that source of the pristine love you already are.

Everything you feel bad, sorrowful, or ashamed about.

Everything that has ever hurt you, or makes you feel bad.

Because if it is not love, it is not you.

And if it doesn't feel good, it is not love, and it doesn't belong to you.

Things like unworthiness, self-doubt, guilt, and shame are all just crap that doesn't belong to us, that has been forced upon us. When we were born, we didn't know what shame, guilt, or self-doubt were. We were just shining. We had to learn how to feel and be and act with shame. Or guilt. Or self-doubt. But it doesn't belong to us. It is *not* us. It is not who we are.

Return this crap to the social matrix. Distance yourself from it. Let it all go. It doesn't matter where you start. Just anything that bothers you and feels uncomfortable—we all have it. Admit that. We all full of crap.

Of course, before I could let go, I also had to realize the truth of this. I had to admit that I was holding onto my past—the personal characteristics that were given to me without asking for them, the need for approval, the need to get more money, and achieve perfection and a lifetime of attachments that never made me truly happy.

Once we do that, we can truly shine. Are you ready? Let's look at how to go about letting go.

11
FIVE SIMPLE LETTING-GO STEPS

Letting go is the process of bursting the mental bubbles that we have been living in for too long. Our constant attachment to the self-stories, external dramas, and never-ending desires takes control of our lives and prevents us from living in the presence of the love we already are. But where does letting go leave us?

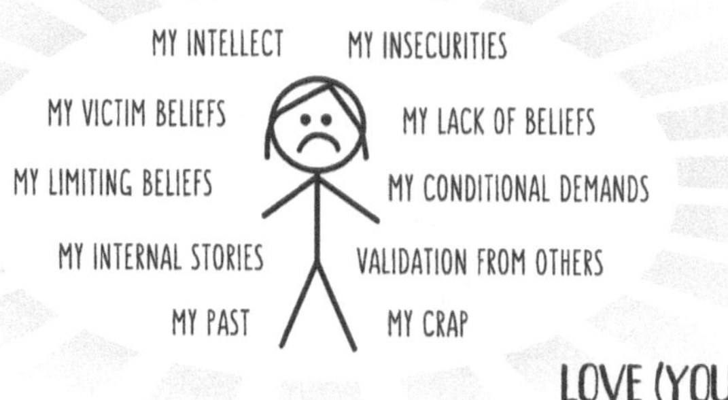

If you let go of ALL your attachments, who will you be WITHOUT them? At least ponder this!

If we open the doors to the love we already are, we will create a new, clean sanctuary where it can settle and stay with us. Instead of trying to fight those controlling bubbles, as I did at first with the Unworthiness bitch, we must melt away the resistance by stripping them of their power. Instead of fighting, we surrender—which is what we do when we let go.

> **Instead of fighting, we surrender—which is what we do when we let go.**

Now, I know this sounds a bit scary. But that's just the reaction of your ego, trying to preserve all those attachments. The ego tries to talk us out of this. It has become comfortable with all that comfortable, old baggage. Now it's afraid of change.

But you need to make a choice: your old stories and the status quo? Or the love you already are? I made my choice when I got fed up with feeling constantly unworthy.

Was it easy?

Hell, no.

Was it life changing?

Hell, yes.

What would my life look like now if I had not taken that leap of faith? Honestly, I don't even want to know. But I can tell you that letting go and surrendering was the beginning of everything for me. So, look at them as positive things.

Also, you are no stranger to them. You have actually been subconsciously letting go already. Just think about some situation in your life when you were so overwhelmed, caught in a negative loop from which you thought you couldn't escape. Maybe it was at work; maybe it was a conflict at home. And then, while seeing no solution, one moment you just threw up your hands and gave up on the situation completely. What happened next?

You surrendered to it, and just let it be. Then, somehow, the problem magically started solving itself!

Why?

Because out of exhaustion, you gave up on the benefit that you thought you could get if you "solved" that bubble. So, the bubble became meaningless to you. You robbed it of its power, and thus it could burst—or at least get much softer!

In other words, you stopped being attached to it.

An attachment to perfection can never bring peace and joy. There always will be something "not good enough." But what happens if we let go of that obsession for perfection? In reality, many (if not most) of our insecurities will disappear as well. The attachment to perfection is nothing more than a coping mechanism for our (self)

beliefs of unworthiness and insecurities flowing from limiting (self) beliefs. Thus, once the bubble of perfection is burst, once being fully detached from it, you will naturally fall into peace, easiness, joy, and love. You are not in this life to prove something to anybody (including yourself). You are here to create, live, and give from the alignment with the love you already are.

That's how paradoxes of life are made. We keep fighting, and nothing happens. Then, we let go and surrender, and things are solved.

We've just been trained to believe that we need to "keep fighting and solving." Nobody ever told us that letting go could be more powerful than fighting. But you knew that intuitively because you were doing it already, in little ways. The love we already are doesn't want us to keep being attached to crap. That's why it sometimes pushes us to extremes, so we finally can let go—so we can burst our mental bubbles and free a space for love. Yes, it often exhausts us, but that's because it is difficult to overcome our stubbornness to preserving our attachments, our stories, our dramas, and our illnesses forever.

So, you see, you already DO have some experience with letting go. You were just not doing it deliberately, and there was not a conscious "system" in it. Well, here is the system that worked for me. It consists of four simple steps that you'll need to practice, plus a "Repeat" step once you are good at those.

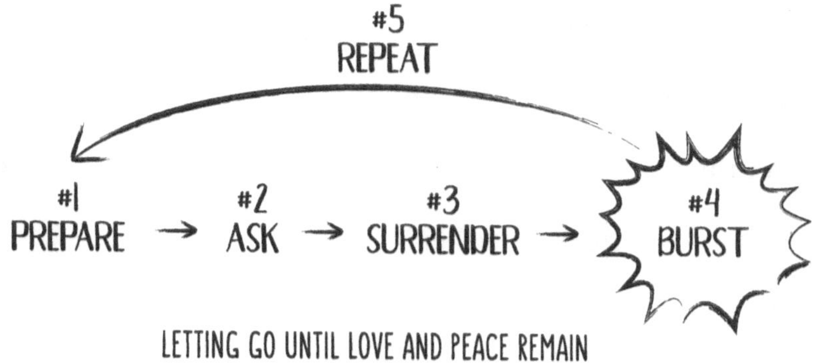

The Letting-Go Process consists of five simple steps, with the "REPEAT" (repetition of the process until the bubble is fully dissolved) as the fifth, optional step.

STEP #1: PREPARE

Find a quiet place. Sit down or lie down (whatever makes you more comfortable) and breathe for one to two minutes to calm the body, and especially, the mind.

Then close your eyes.

Feel relaxed.

Watch the flow of your emotions, thoughts, and images in your head—but do NOT engage with them. Remain totally detached from them.

Just observe, and for three to five minutes, do nothing.

Do NOT want anything from those thoughts, feelings, and images.

Do NOT engage.

Stay in this calm observation mode.

Let them be exactly as they are.

Move your attention to heart.

Try to open it more.

STEP #2: ASK

After a few minutes, when you feel more detached from all your daily activities and from anything that your mind still could be producing to try to get your attention, ask yourself a question:

What is stopping me from realizing that I am endless potential and love?

Or:

Why am I not living in an endless abundance of love yet?

Or any of these more straightforward questions:

Why can't I love myself unconditionally?

What is my current mental bubble?

What I am holding on to?

What is my strongest attachment?

Continue with whatever comes to your mind *naturally, spontaneously*. Try what works best for you. This may be a bit different each time, so don't be afraid to generate similar questions. The exact wording is not that important! What's truly important is:

- having a strong and authentic inner *intention* to let go of ANY of your crap
- being connected to your *heart* during the process, not to your mind
- being very open-minded and not expecting anything in particular.

Then, WAIT. And PAY ATTENTION.

In a few moments, you will notice some mental "bubbles" arising.

Now, VERY, VERY IMPORTANT:

These bubbles will be in the form of feelings and emotions, rather than specific words. You will literally start feeling like some kind of emotional bubble is taking over.

For example:

- You had a very busy day. A strong sensation of hardship arises.
- You had a fight with your partner. A strong feeling of not being lovable arises.
- Nothing happened through the entire day, and a strong feeling of boredom arises.
- You feel alone on this day, and a strong feeling of loneliness arises.

Sometimes, the feeling that arises might have NOTHING to do with your actual day. So, allow the bubbles to surface without wondering exactly what they are. Do NOT look for any mind-created connection. Just allow.

For example:

- An unexpected feeling of unworthiness arises out of the blue.
- An unexpected old memory returns, together with many different feelings.
- The feelings that arise are rather confusing, so the main feeling is exactly that, confusion.
- A sudden feeling of guilt arises, and you feel like crying (so just cry!).

If the feeling kindles a strong sensation in some part of your body (like your heart), then narrow your focus to that area, but keep that overall feeling before you.

It's important to NOT suppress anything. And at the same time, do NOT force anything. Let your heart and your higher intelligence know exactly where to find you. Just stay open, and let arise exactly what is supposed to arise.

Do not waste your time trying to connect the feelings to some story or mind-created description. Just ALLOW everything and do not block anything. Be sure not to push the feelings away (you have been doing it for too long already, that's why we need to work on them now.)

In the beginning, you might find this practice strange, but with time, you will get used to it.

STEP #3: SURRENDER

Now, SURRENDER to that mix of feelings.

Just let them wash over you.

Let them overwhelm you.

They have been suppressed for too long, and the only way to get rid of them is to finally ALLOW them.

I know, it sounds counterintuitive, but that's how it works.

Don't worry about discomfort. It will only last a few seconds or minutes. Instead, embrace the discomfort. Allow anything. If you feel like crying, cry. If you feel like laughing, laugh. Whatever the bubble, allow yourself to stay in it for a little while. These feelings need to be experienced; otherwise, they'll never go away.

STEP #4: BURST

And finally, once you are fully surrendered to the feeling behind that certain mental and emotional "bubble" …

RELEASE IT.

Say in your mind:

I don't need this bubble anymore. It doesn't serve me in becoming who I truly am—pure love.

And imagine the bubble BURSTING.

If you have difficulties popping that bubble, then imagine you are simply STEPPING OUT of it. Then turn back, look at the bubble sharply, and let that knife-sharp gaze BURST that bubble.

Once you fully "feel" your bubble, then step out of it (in your imagination), turn back to it, and let it burst. Then, have a look around (in your imagination again) to see if you immediately enter some bigger bubble, within which the smaller one was burst. This happens. If so, repeat the whole process: Feel into that bubble, step out of it, and let it go. Keep going like that until you can do this easily. The more bubbles you destroy, the more you'll let go of years' worth of limiting beliefs and accumulated crap.

And then ... you will feel an indescribable RELIEF.

With the bubble gone, years of emotional burden will disappear in a fraction of a second.

You will feel AMAZING.

You will feel at peace. Free of that bubble. Finally.

STEP #5: REPEAT

Repeat this process a few more times, if you like. Usually, there is more than one layer of bubbles. You'll have your work cut out for you! Each time you burst a bubble, check and see if the feeling of it is still there. If it does remain, the feeling will be much weaker.

But even that needs to be let go of. So get back to Step #3 (Surrender), and repeat.

Sometimes you'll need to repeat the task a few times, and that is good. That means you are letting go of something really serious and important.

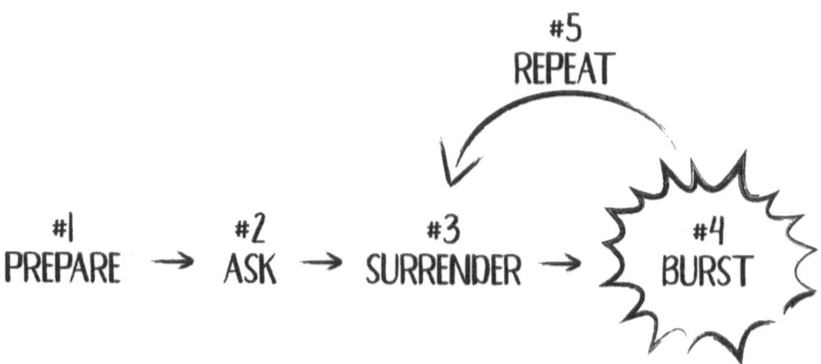

It is usually good practice to repeat the whole process a couple of times in one session. Once you burst your bubble, just see if there is another one, or if you aren't already located in some bigger one. Then go back to Step #3, surrender to it, and burst it again. Keep repeating (Step #5) until you succeed, or until you notice more bubbles. (Important note: If you feel there is already "nothing" to burst, then bear in mind that even "nothingness" is a bubble that can be burst. Feel encouraged moving through these abstract bubbles too; they are just as important to let go of as more specific bubbles).

Now, one more important thing. Don't worry too much about whether you did it "right." If you used your intuition, it will be right, in most cases. Do not try to do this "perfectly." There is no "perfect" way of letting go. And if you still need the "perfect" guidance and the final confirmation you did it "right and perfectly," then start with letting go of your "perfection" mental bubble. This will make both the process and your life much easier!

Just keep going. Practice. After a few trials, it will become really easy and highly intuitive. You'll be able to do the Letting-Go Process nearly anywhere, and often almost subconsciously. All it requires is a bit of patience, dedication, and training.

Now, I would like to share with you a deeper taste of the Letting-Go Process. In 2016, I did a very powerful letting-go session with my friend and a top athlete, Brandon. (I guided him through the entire process, which is also something I do at my "You Are Love" retreats.) He was so overwhelmed with the immediate result, that he recorded a short video about it. You will find a link to it in the FREE bonus section at <u>www. YouAreLoveBook.com/love</u>. But here is a transcript of it.

Source: www.LettingGoMovement.com

Brandon: Welcome guys to Letting Go. Guys, Letting Go is an experience that has been worth waiting for, for me personally.

I got to experience letting go for the first time on the top of a mountain at a Buddhist temple with Tomas, the founder of Letting Go, and he wanted to share this experience with me.

Which I was skeptical of at first, I got to say. I mean, I've heard lots and lots of different types of healings and spiritual experiences that people can have and, you know, I was doubtful and then without really knowing what I was doing, I was letting go of the fact that I had doubts. I let go of these thoughts and I led myself to experience.

Within the process, when I got there on the top of the mountain with Tomas, we sat there and he went through the process with me.

At first, I closed my eyes. Everyone has their own way of doing it. I closed my eyes, I absorbed the moment, what was going on, how I was feeling, allowed myself to feel, I just stopped all distraction. As he took me through the process, I just became lighter and lighter and lighter.

My problems were going away, my fears were going away, my confidence in myself was growing, and even when I got to the point of feeling so confident and just free, I even let that go.

That was quite an experience for me because I originally thought that that was what I was supposed to do is be so confident and powerful, but it's more than that.

Letting go of that ego, which for me, that's something that's plagued me, it was incredible.

Can't really go more into it unless you experience it first hand, but it's worth a try, and I urge everybody to allow yourself to experience the process of letting go.

You will see it and you will certainly appreciate it. Just keep an open mind, and we look forward to spending some time with you.

12

REAL-LIFE LETTING-GO PROCESS EXAMPLE

In 2016, Maria and I went through several Letting-Go Processes together and recorded them. You can watch the entire video as a FREE bonus at www.YouAreLoveBook. com/love. I include the translated transcript here, as a real-life case study, along with some important, practical comments.

(We were already relaxed, so before we started, Step #1: Prepare had been already done.)

Tomas: Okay. We'll have another demonstration. Let's try some other way to express feeling and let it go. Let it disappear, once and for all.

Okay, Maria, *what's a kind of feeling that you really don't like, that bothers you a lot?* A feeling that you have in everyday life?

(That was Step #2: Ask. We were taking advantage of the momentum and allowing anything to arise that was supposed to arise. You can use the question we used in this example too.)

Maria: Not being myself.

Tomas: Okay.

Maria: Not being true to the person who I am deep inside and pretending that I'm someone else just to please others before I please myself.

Tomas: How does it feel?

(Now we are going deeper into that feeling, so it can be experienced fully.)

Maria: Horrible. It feels like I always come last, and not only to myself but for everybody, because I don't consider myself important enough to be cared about. If I don't feel that way toward myself, how will others relate to me? Why would I be important to anybody else?

Tomas: Where do you feel it?

(I just asked to see if the feeling was stronger in some part of the body. Sometimes it is, sometimes it is not.)

Maria: In my heart.

Tomas: Can you step into this feeling in your heart?

(Once the location of the source of the feeling is noticed, we need to refocus there.)

Maria: I don't really want to.

(This is normal. It takes some courage to dive into our own crap!)

Tomas: Can you, for the purpose of letting it go, at least try? What do you feel?

(Now we are really surrendering to that. This is Step #3.)

Maria: It's sadness. Sadness, knowing that I could have done so much more with my life, and also that the people I love, they are not getting the full emotions and love that I could share with them. That's what I feel.

Tomas: Is there some other feeling behind this sadness?

(Sometimes you can sift through the layers sooner or later in the process; you just need to experiment with what works best for you. In this example, I was just going with the present moment.)

Maria: Yeah.

Tomas: What is that?

Maria: That fear of not being lovable enough. That I always have to be someone to get love or to experience love. Yeah.

Tomas: Can you step into this feeling and feel it all over your body right now? Whatever it does mean, however it feels, can you just let the feeling express itself, and can you slowly let it go? Can you tell yourself, "I don't want this feeling anymore. This feeling doesn't belong to me. This feeling is not part of who I am, and you're allowed to let this feeling go, disappear."?

(Here we are first surrendering even deeper, and then we are moving to Step #4: Burst.)

Maria: It's just been so long.

Tomas: Can you let it go?

Maria: Yes.

Tomas: Can you feel the energy behind that?

Maria: Yes.

Tomas: Can you feel how it's disappearing?

(This is a gentle way to suggest to burst the bubble. With some people, I would need to be more direct. However, Maria was a very sensitive and gentle woman, so I had to go through the process with her accordingly.)

Maria: Yeah.

Tomas: What does it feel like? Tell it to the camera.

Maria: It feels free. It feels light. It feels like I'm lifted. It feels like now I can actually experience life. I can go out there, and I can just spread the love that I have inside, instead of being someone who is restricting all these feelings, not just from myself but also from others. It's easy. It's being easy with life.

Tomas: Would you like to try it? Would you like letting go of all your fears?

Maria: Try it. It's all worth it.

Note: Themes like this (unworthiness, unlovability) are very common and very deeply rooted. So, they usually are not fully resolved during one Letting-Go Process session only. They tend to return, so they can be let go of repeatedly, again and again. Each time, they become softer, and over months, they can disappear completely, even if they had been bothering you for decades before.

13

HOW TO USE THE LETTING-GO PROCESS IN DAILY LIFE

Before we move forward to another purification method, let me close this first one with a few more important thoughts.

First, although you can and probably will have some profound experiences and shifts after just a few Letting-Go Process sessions (as did some of my friends whom I guided through this process), you need to have a lot of patience and persistence too. And you have to really want it.

My realization of the love we already are through the Letting-Go Process was driven by a relentless desire to go further and deeper. Without desire, without curiosity, without the thorough intention to go deep, I would probably just create another mental bubble called "pretending I am bursting my bubbles" while, in fact, I was staying in the bubble of comfort and "safety" and thus not moving anywhere. It would be just another bubble inside of the "comfort" bubble.

It takes a lot of practice to start TRULY shifting your life. One or two sessions will not be enough. I had to do hundreds of them and be very patient because with many of them it felt like nothing was solved, nothing happened. Other times, I had breakthroughs. But I couldn't predict when that would happen, so to start truly moving forward, I had to learn to let go of one especially important bubble: the "need for immediate results" bubble.

The profusion of bubbles can, indeed, get pretty complex and tricky to navigate. Even if you feel "stuck" with the Letting-Go Process, you later realize that "stuckness" is a bubble too! And the reason why you felt "stuck" during the letting-go session was just to realize this bubble and let it go of it too (and this bubble will especially arise if you feel stuck in your entire life.)

The maze of your mind, the complexity of the crap you are full of, will surprise you again and again. But that is another important reason why you need to keep going and letting go, by any means. Keep purifying yourself from as many bubbles as possible, so you can start dropping more and more into your heart and slowly opening the door to the love you already are, wider and wider.

Nobody else will do this for you, and it can only be achieved with practice. So, you need to let go of the typical consumer's comfort and laziness, and go all in, if you TRULY desire to shift your life into amazing fulfillment and magic. Be patient! This will probably take months, or even years (although you will have some very fast and visible results too!)

Yet, it is still worth it. Every minute of letting go counts and moves you closer toward a much better and happier life. The good news is that once you practice the Letting-Go Process a few times, it will almost become automatic. One day, you'll be able to do it in your car, while stuck in traffic, on a city bus, in a cinema, or even during a business meeting!

Once you are all in, and keep practicing, it gets easier and easier. I had times when I felt that the whole day was just one big letting-go—and I didn't feel I had to put in much effort.

So, keep going. Keep practicing. Make it a habit. Don't complicate it, don't overthink it; just do it from your heart in the first place. It feels good.

You can get more examples and tools in the FREE bonus section at www.YouAreLoveBook.com/love. So, keep going and letting go of your crap. You have acquired so much of it during your life. Th rough those dark clouds, no wonder it is so hard for the love you already are to shine fully!

14
STEP #2:
FREE EMOTIONAL FLOW

Now you know the process behind my very first encounter of the love we already are. It is powerful and life-changing. But that is definitely not the only entry point to the love you already are. Nor are the bubbles of your crap the only thing you need to learn how to purify and detach from.

The next one is your EMOTIONS. Don't freak out yet! Let's start from the beginning.

During the last few years, I have been profoundly interested in learning about as many ways to let go as possible. I always treated this practically: since the very first encounter with the love we all already are, I simply wanted to know how to get to this amazing space again, faster, easier, and ultimately, to stay there permanently. And I never cared what it took.

Since Day 1, there was an honest desire, as well as readiness for any experiments, including those that many would call "extreme." If that meant faster results, I was all for it! So, what

I am going to share with you next is what I found as the most intense way to the direct realization of the love you already are.

In fact, I love this technique more and more, and practice it as often as possible. My goal is to make it a "permanent state of my being" this year. But I have to warn you: it can really get pretty intense!

At the beginning of 2018, I spent three months in one of my favorite cities in the world, Kuala Lumpur, the capital of Malaysia. I was working on this book there, as well as going through the "self-love" surveys that I did with seven hundred people, to understand better how to help people with their blocks toward experiencing more self-love. One day, I was sitting in my favorite coffee shop when I noticed a guy staring at me. Given his demeanor, he appeared to be gay.

Now, I am definitely not a gay (far from it, actually), and I felt uncomfortable about his staring at me the way he was. I ignored him, but I could still sense his stare—I could feel it even behind my back. I really needed to focus on my research, so I decided to leave and move to another coffee shop, on the other side of the street.

But while I was walking over there, I started thinking about my emotions (which I do quite often, to better understand how we people operate and react emotionally). I wondered:

Why was I (or this body, more precisely) feeling uncomfortable? The man was not threatening me (the body) in any way directly.

Why are we so sensitive to discomfort? What would happen if I stood in that discomfort? What emotion would come next? Would that be acceptance, more anxiety, or something completely different?

Why do people constantly manage emotions, instead of allowing them to be exactly as they are?

And then it finally struck me.

Is managing our emotions the right thing to do?

I know it sounds crazy. Everybody is doing that, right? But nearly everybody is also NOT fully aligned to the source of the love we all already are.

And as we have seen, in order to experience more of the source of the love we already are in our lives, we need to learn how to ALLOW. Including our emotions—any, or rather, ALL of them!

Of course, on a practical level, this idea, alone, made me uncomfortable. And of course, I immediately started "managing" that emotion, by trying to pull myself out of the whole idea. But my intuition was dragging me back, and because I have high confidence in my instincts, especially since the very first encounter with the love we all are, I knew I was onto something!

So, I continued thinking:

How can we ever be AUTHENTIC if all we are trying to do for most of our lives is MANAGE EMOTIONS, without even thinking about it?

Of course, a big part of the answer is the social, religious, and cultural conditioning imposed on us, usually without consent, that forces us to behave certain ways. On top of that, there are also past experiences and our moral belief systems. So, I dug deeper:

How much are we actually SACRIFICING for these constructs? What if true authenticity is MORE than what we were programmed to blindly believe we should do and how we should act in any given moment?

And then it hit me:

What if our past experiences don't matter at all? What if we are wrong? What if managing emotions is, in fact, the STUPIDEST thing we can do, because it is nothing more than continual suppression?

What if our past experiences don't matter at all? What if we are wrong?

Of course, had I not had my direct experiences with the results of ALLOWANCE and AUTHENTICITY, I would probably never ask these questions. I was now able to distinguish between true authenticity (which is heart-based) and pretended authenticity and complete inauthenticity (which is mind and ego driven), in both myself and others.

At that time, I was craving true authenticity like never before because I was on a path of deep realization that dropping all our shields is BETTER and EASIER, and can bring more amazing stuff and experiences in our lives—despite having been programmed otherwise.

I got excited by these questions because I could feel there was something very truthful about them. For most people, these questions would be highly uncomfortable, but that friction is what inspired me to investigate deeper. Because only behind the programmed pretending can the authentic truth be discovered.

So, that day, February 11, 2018, I decided to find the truth. I would try this insane experiment:

Not managing any of my emotions and letting them be exactly as they are for a few days.

No exceptions. I would start fresh the next day.

15

SEVEN DAYS OF EMOTIONAL HELL

DAY ONE

On February 12, 2018, I woke up and started with the experiment. It was a regular workday. I was not on vacation; I had a bunch of routine work to manage, along with some demanding tasks. These would be tough to handle even WITH managing emotions, yet, I decided NOT to manage any on that day.

The goal was not to be driven by them, but rather let them be as they were. I would not manage them, rationalize them, nor try to change them. I would simply do NOTHING about them.

ALLOWANCE.

AUTHENTICITY.

To help myself, I made very specific rules that I decided to follow for that day:

1) No blocking, pushing back, or managing anything.

2) No reacting to anything.

3) No labeling, no prioritizing. I would see all the emotions equally, simply as they were. I would connect to their "is-ness", rather than their meaning. I would not say, "This emotion is bad" or "This one is good" (labeling). I would not prioritize in the sense that "I don't want this emotion; it feels uncomfortable. Let's refocus on a different one."

4) No giving meaning or stories to any emotions. I would not say, "This emotion means this or that and exists because of that."

Well, it is very hard to tell you what the first day was like, but it was a true HELL.

I had never realized before how much we suppress emotions during a normal day. That alone is a reason for you to do a similar experiment: to see just how often we are inauthentic and untrue to ourselves.

In fact, I gauged it to be about 90 percent of the time, if not even more. We are, during that time, just pretending. We play silly games while pretending to be authentic, but only by the measure of the image and idea in our mind, about what "authentic" should or could probably look like. We manipulate ourselves (behavior, speech) into appearing in the eyes of others as "authentic"—which is actually an artificial, mind-created self-image used to get more positive validation from others. But we rarely experience emotion that comes from heart, where the TRUE authenticity comes from. And we don't even care; we let our programs override our true, natural, authentic expression.

In simple terms, it means that 90 percent of the day, we are NOT who we really are.

In addition, I decided to do one more crazy thing: to document the whole experiment on the Internet, on a Facebook page, and share it with other people. I wrote:

The first day could be described as a "living hell" (although I would prefer no labeling, in this case, I think it is relevant.) Something like being in an interrogation room, where you are constantly, heavily beaten by a "bad cop" to confess to something you have never done, while a "good cop" tells you, "Calm down. We haven't even started yet." In the evening, I was totally exhausted, and I am glad I survived.

That first day of stopping managing emotions is really cruel. All that heavy crap you have been suppressing for years finally gets the chance to surface and express itself. This internal garbage lets you know that it exists, and it wants to be free.

Believe me, the amount of suppressed emotions within us is insane. After this experience, I don't wonder why people are sick. Why cancer exists. Why people collapse and have heart attacks.

Somehow, I survived. But sadly, at the end of the day, besides great emotional exhaustion (and confusion too), nothing more was there, nothing I could derive some conclusion from, or say I learned something from.

So, I decided to keep being crazy. I decided to extend this insanity one more day (yes, deliberately entering the hell again).

Tomas Nesnidal
February 13

\#transformation \#awareness \#acceptance \#selfrealization \#experiment

Ok, so last two days I did a really crazy experiment:
I STOPPED MANAGING ANY EMOTIONS.

I simply decided to allow all the emotions to be exactly as they are for 2 entire days. Let them live as they appear, without pushing anything back, without managing them, or reacting to them.

The "rules" were like this:
1) No blocking, pushing back, or managing anything.
2) No reacting to anything.
3) No labeling, no prioritizing - seeing all the emotions equally, simply as they are, or rather, to connect to their "is-ness", rather than meaning. Not saying "this emotion is bad" or "this one is good" (labeling), no prioritizing in sense "I don't want this emotion, it feels uncomfortable, let's refocus to a different one".
4) No giving meaning or stories to any emotions (not saying "this emotion means this or that and is because of that).

DAY TWO

The second day was a similar descent into hell, but there was some easiness at the end of the day that had not been there before. I described it on Facebook that day like this:

The second day was similar, but somehow NOT resisting anything felt easier, more ok, more "peaceful". During the whole day, I felt an enormous pressure on my chest (I was literally worried if an alien would all of sudden jump out of my chest). In the evening, I felt like I would collapse every minute. But I survived again.

Again, no conclusions, no lessons to learn. I went to bed with absolute exhaustion, and the next day, I finally started to feel some relief. Again, I made some Facebook notes:

Today, I feel EMPTY. Just empty, that's it. Not fully empty, but empty. Which could be considered as a bit of relief compared to

the last two days, but again – I don't want to prioritize because instinctively I feel I shouldn't.

DAYS THREE TO SIX

Since it seemed to be working, even though the experience was painful, I kept at it. You have no idea how much you have been suppressing your entire life, for no reason or benefit. Once you ALLOW these emotions to finally be, they will completely overwhelm you. There are TOO MANY of them.

Yes, it hurt to let them wash over me, but how else would I disperse them? And how important was it to do so? Just imagine how much energy and effort it costs you all the time, again, for nothing! The only benefit you can get out of it is an illness, disease, or heart attack!

On Day 4, I woke up crying. I got literally, seriously depressed. Or, let's put it the right way. *I* was not depressing myself. Too many suppressed negative emotions were coming to the surface, bringing with them a feeling of depression. But that is an emotion too, and that needs to be allowed too—if we want to cleanse ourselves from it.

That morning, I felt like I was locked within billions of emotions that I'd been suppressing for decades. Now, when I opened them up, they totally got me. But I finally wanted to ALLOW them, I wanted to be authentic, not to pretend anymore. The immediate result felt like hell had decided to punish me for that experiment!

I felt like I would die every minute. I didn't think I could handle any more. An indescribable feeling of SAMENESS also arose! I don't know where it came from or why it was there, but it just was! I kept my Facebook description short, as I had no strength to write more:

Tomas Nesnidal DAY 4 OF THE EXPERIMENT: I woke up crying.

Acceptance sucks.

I woke up with a horrible feeling and thought: What if acceptance means "sameness".

After all that path of trying to make your life better, fill it with unconditional love and kindness, you realize it is not happening. Nothing seems working, you still seem to be stuck in the same reality, the same place. Whatever you do, whatever you try - still the same thing, still the same "sameness".

So what if this is what you need to accept too.

This sameness.

The thought that this will be here until the end of your body life.

The idea and possibility nothing will EVER change, whatever you do.

But acceptance means you need to accept all the feelings and thoughts, including this.

This was really hard and I was crying the whole morning. It feels like this: you so much want something different, but all you are left with is to accept more of the current.

I did my best.

I am somehow more and more apathetic. Whatever.

It doesn't feel frustrating or hopeless.

It just sucks.

Acceptance really sucks.

But I feel there is no other way, I am really determined to go through this.

Love and good luck to all of you. 

Like   Reply · 12w    5

On that horrible day, when I couldn't bear any more, I finally surrendered.

Because there was nothing else I could do.

I felt like I could not get back, nor ahead.

I felt like I could do NOTHING, I was totally stuck.

The only option, out of all options, was to ACCEPT that. So, I did.

Still, the hell continued for several more days. Somehow, I still had to live a normal working and social life. But I couldn't stop. I wasn't able to. And I don't even remember much about those next days, except that it was a true week of living hell.

Then, it finally happened.

DAY SEVEN

On Day 7, I woke up, and the pain was gone. All that remained was:

... the bliss of the love we already are in its amazing power, back again.

Fully present. Overwhelming me. And it was pouring and pouring and pouring.... I felt so at peace.

With myself.

With others.

With my past.

With my present.

With people.

With this entire Universe.

At last, I was enjoying all those beautiful feelings of unconditional, Universal love and acceptance that were finally flowing, intensely, beautifully. Later on, I made my last post about what happens when we stop managing our emotions:

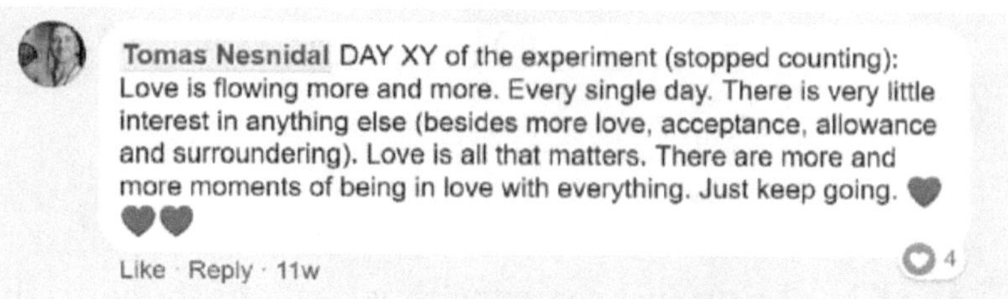

We are nothing but love. And we are not only constantly hiding it behind our crap, but also behind our emotional inauthenticity. I learned that there is no benefit in trying to manage our emotions. In letting them be, we—and they—are free.

16

WITH FREE EMOTIONAL FLOW, I PROMISE YOU A MIRACLE

What I have just shared with you might sound frightening, but the end result was nothing less than a true purification miracle. Yes, my very first experience with this experiment was a bit shaky, and yes, it might have been a bit extreme. But when everything settled down, I had to admit that it was one of the most freeing things I have ever done in my life.

We constantly think how smart and "skillful" we are if we learn to "manage our emotions". But in truth, that is nothing more than another form of pretending. It is just another way of manipulating ourselves, while covering up our full authenticity.

Who says we need to "manage emotions" instead of staying truthful to what we are?

What's so wrong with being authentic?

Who says we need to "manage emotions" instead of staying truthful to what we are? If others have a problem with our authenticity, that's THEIR problem, not ours. Perhaps being ourselves will inspire them to start being more authentic too.

The majority of people have such closed hearts that when somebody else is authentic and truthful, it causes insecurity. They don't know how to react to that. They try to handle the situation with mind and brain, but it can only be embraced by heart.

Now, understand this clear distinction: I am not talking about being EMOTIONAL. That's fine. I am talking about you *not managing* emotions, letting them all be exactly as they are in the given moment, and lovingly embracing them. These are two very different things, and one needs to come through the experiment I did to fully realize it. So, give it a try.

Yes, in the beginning, you will feel so "marinated" in this emotional stew that you'll feel like you might explode. But even that is just an emotion. Don't react to it; allow it to be exactly as it is. You can still go through a regular day while not managing a single emotion. And people likely will not even notice.

If you persist with this experiment through several days, you will start feeling more and more authentic. You will start feeling more and more truthful, to yourself as well as the people around you. You will also feel a bit (or even very) vulnerable, but that is okay. That's your heart opening. Embrace that too.

When this authenticity bubbles up you will feel connected, like the TRUE you. You'll want to hug yourself for how innocent and beautiful you are, despite all the past social programming, regrets, false stories, self-doubts, and irrelevant personal opinions that so many inauthentic people held about you in the past. That's because this authenticity is also a form of the love you already are, talking through you, through and with your heart.

Of course, this will cause a few sudden emotional reactions, like crying, for example. There may be tears caused by past suppressed pains being released, or the pain of the vulnerability you don't yet know how to handle, or the sensation of your heart opening wildly (I still don't know why it feels painful sometimes, but it just does, and there's no need to question it.) Now, these are the moments I was talking about that can make another person feel uncomfortable.

But that's totally okay. You are not here to make others comfortable. You are here to shine your authentic you, shine the love you already are, so it can touch other people's hearts and inspire them to start opening theirs too.

Stop covering up, pretending, and playing roles, just because other people want you to. Be your authentic you, pouring directly from your wildly opened, beautiful heart. You'll be able to stop "prioritizing" emotions, saying that this is better than that and this is what you allow yourself to feel now, or this is what you don't. You'll see all the emotions equally—like LOVE. Or an EXPRESSION of love.

Once you do this, they will all unify into love.

And because you will be the very center of this field, your heart will start opening tremendously. Love will start pouring through your whole body and existence, without anybody or anything causing it. So, stop being afraid of your emotions, and do this exercise with a smile on your lips. Do it at your pace— gently or "all in" (like me). It is up to you. But do it. I am here to tell you that you will come through it, stronger than before. You will feel liberated, you will feel light, you will feel taken care of by life, with kindness, gentleness, and love. You will start being absorbed in the love, beauty, and perfection you already are.

Since my first "all in" experiment, I haven't done it so extremely again, but I do this purification gently nearly every single day. At least for a few hours a day, I let myself be fully immersed in my emotions. I see them as love. I don't label them. I don't react to them. I don't rationalize them or make stories out of them, I just allow them to be exactly as they are. Whenever I do this with absolute honesty and surrender to it fully, I feel *incredible*.

Like being in love, making love, looking into eyes of the infinity of love—but with my own soul. Like being authentic and vulnerable, yet feeling absolutely invincible. Like being very, very intimate, yet more connected to others and to this world than ever.

You are NOT your emotions.

You are pure love.

17

SOMETHING I'VE NEVER SHARED WITH ANYONE

I trust you. I have confidence in you. I know you are pristine love, that is why I am going to share with you something that I've never told anyone.

When I was going through this extreme experiment of not managing any emotions, for a few days I also was living in extreme, unpleasant, and frustrating sexual desire. But as part of the experiment, I did not react to it; I let it be exactly as it was. I accepted it lovingly. I allowed it to exist, and witnessed it without any bias or controlling impulses.

Of course, it was not easy. It was pretty new to me, but again, I was curious to see what would happen if I *didn't* react. Interestingly, as I allowed these feelings, I became aware of the deep collective sexual suppression humans have lived with through the ages. This suppression came about through social conditioning, religious persuasion, commercial manipulation, sexploitation, and much more. But that is a topic for another book.

It was not pleasant, it was like all this history of sexual suppression, oppression, manipulation, and abuse of all of mankind pouring on/through me. In fact, it was pretty hard to handle and digest.

As difficult as these new realizations were, I still allowed the feelings to be as they were, without any judgment (who am I to judge, anyway?). Absolute allowance, just as love is unconditional.

And then, in a moment when I thought I couldn't handle a single bit more:

... all that energy released.

And it was one of the weirdest moments of my life! It felt like all of the sexual desires of my existence had been satisfied at once. I seemed to be in perfect harmony with the highest feminine sensibility, as though both the pure masculine and pure feminine were flowing through me and merging together.

Then, all the intensity was replaced with peace.

I felt like I was both a man and a woman simultaneously. I could be and feel both the polarities at the same time, and merge them as much as I wanted. There was zero conflict between the masculine and feminine, just a beautiful blend of both, and omnipresent perfection.

Then, all the intensity was replaced with a peace.

It felt extremely natural, authentic and truthful—in direct contrast with what society taught us to believe about the distinct energies between men and women. Each enriched the other, in an infinite, upward spiral of harmony and perfection.

I felt like ONE.

It felt pretty confusing (a lot of social programming in the background was still going on), but pretty incredible as well. I was a bit scared of it, too, so I did not let it grow and actually started managing it a bit. But I felt a definite alignment.

This experience, alone, was worth every second of that few days of emotional hell. I never shared this on the Facebook group, as I felt a bit ashamed (again, a result of social programming). But today, with distance and in retrospect, I can see that there is really nothing to hide from "others." That's because there are no others. We are all one, coming from the same source of unconditional love.

So, you see, purification from your suppressed emotions is much more than a difficult exercise.

There can be a lot of fun too! :-)

18

STEP #3: MINDLESS LOVE

So, you already know you are not your crap. Nor your emotions. How could you even ever be them, if those are just things that appear and then disappear?

Anything that just comes and goes is not you. How could it be? Only the love you already are is you. Our goal is to make that as obvious and present to you as possible. Let me share a short story with you.

At the end of 2016, quite a while after my first realization of the love we already are, and endless *letting-gos* later, I realized I was burnt out from my work. I had been running a highly profitable business in the Czech Republic with my business partner and friend for almost ten years, yet it somehow made less and less sense to continue doing that. I felt I was supposed to do something more aligned to my deep realizations of the love we are and to my true life purpose. I wanted to do something meaningful, something that could help this planet and bring the people living on it to a better, happier, more connected, kinder, and more loving place.

So, at the end of that year, I decided to quit the company and sell all my shares.

A lot of people thought that I was crazy to quit a business that very likely could keep financing my comfortable life. But I didn't crave that safety anymore. Or, at least not as much as before. I wanted to deeply know who I really am and why I am here. I wanted to know **I wanted to deeply know who I really am and why I am here.** how to exchange a "safe" life for a "spectacular" life, one in which I could give to others and inspire them to do so.

All of a sudden, I did not feel driven by money or success or validation (these bubbles were, in many cases, gone already) but rather by inspiration, love, connection, contribution, and a deeper sense of purpose. So, at the beginning of 2017, I did all the necessary paperwork to get rid of my company shares, said "bye-bye" to the comfort and safety, and leapt into the unknown.

I started by taking a break and traveling, going to amazing concerts like U2 in Barcelona, and visiting some retreats that could help me clarify my purpose and deepen my realizations of the love we all come from. So, it happened that one day I ended up in the Netherlands, at a retreat held by Bentinho Massaro. I learned more from this experience than from all my efforts in the previous few years combined.

But, my true journey had started already, a few days ahead of that!

It was during a hot July, in a Netherlands' city called Eindhoven, where I met a young woman named Lorelle. We were both on our way to the retreat. We started talking and immediately clicked.

She, too, had an incredible desire to realize higher truths, a desire for the direct self-realization of the unconditional love we already are, for connection and for manifestation of life purpose. She, too, was willing to experiment crazily and go "all in," despite the need for safety and comfort, despite any fears or self-doubts. She was truly a heart-driven and heart-opened being (still pretty rare to meet nowadays).

We had one full free day before the retreat, so we decided to go into the center of the city, sit on a bench, and meditate a bit together on a question: "*What is it that we want to get from that retreat?*"

The meditation itself was an incredible experience. When we started, it was still morning, the street was completely empty, and we were the only ones there. So, we closed our eyes and started meditating. It was a highly "emptying" experience: for me, it felt like I was not just clearing my mind, but wiping everything out of my consciousness. I felt a completely empty presence, where nothing bothered me, nothing seemed to be, and yet the emptiness was extremely satisfying.

I remained in this state for twenty or thirty minutes, and when Lorelle and I opened our eyes again, pretty much at the same time, we couldn't believe what we saw:

We were literally surrounded by a CROWD of people!

It was almost a blizzard: the bench where just the two of us had been sitting when we began meditating was now crammed full, occupied by six or seven more people. We had not noticed them arrive, even though there were so many, right next to us, on the small bench.

In addition, a group of people stood nearby, surrounding the bench, even though the rest of the street was still empty and the neighboring benches were vacant. It was as if all the passers-by on the street had suddenly, for no good reason, gathered around "our" bench. I looked at Lorelle and asked:

"What do you feel right now, with all these people around?"

And we both, almost simultaneously, replied:

"Emptiness."

As if the people weren't even there! As if the street wasn't there. As if WE weren't even there. It was bizarre—a complete emptiness, despite the visual fullness of the place. It was really like inhabiting some kind of dream.

Now, from thousands of previous meditations and letting-go processes, I was pretty much used to anything, but this was totally new to me. We sat for a while longer, to absorb the whole experience, and then we agreed to walk a bit. As we did, the sensation did not change. It felt like we were in a movie, where nothing was real (including us) and everything was empty of meaning. It just WAS. Nothing less, nothing more.

So we decided to play with that experience a bit more. We tried different ways of interacting with the surroundings, but whatever we did, we always ended up with the realization that, at that moment, EVERYTHING was completely empty of meaning. Not meaningless in a bad or assaulting way, but meaningless that WAS, with no other quality to it.

Yes, we felt connected to it, so it was not like ignorance or apathy—it was different than that. It was like a lucid dream, and we couldn't make deeper sense of it. We were free to just enjoy it and stood in the experience until it disappeared (which I think was for about an hour.)

Now, let's get back to the very beginning. Recall that we started with a simple question:

"What is it that we want to get from that retreat?"

On the train to Baarlo, the site of the retreat, Lorelle and I talked this over, and we concluded that we had shared this experience because what we both really wanted to gain from the retreat was:

Emptiness!

We wanted to hit the RESET button of our *minds*, to experience what we are like WITHOUT mind.

We both knew from past individual experiences that emptying the mind is the fastest way to deeper realizations and reconnection with heart and the love we already are. Yet, neither of us knew exactly how to do this. How to detach not only from our crap and emotions but also our minds—at least for a few seconds!

"Mind" equals past stories, descriptions, memories, rationalization, and logic, and it is all just a distraction from who we truly are. From the love we already are. So, why not try to detach from it a bit too? Why not empty it sometimes, as much as we can? Empty the recycle bin, clear our cache.

Lorelle and I both wanted to know what the space BEYOND mind is.

That was our theme.

We instinctively KNEW we are not our minds, those containers full of stories, programming, and rubbish, and we wanted to know who we are WITHOUT that, what the reality feels like. We just didn't know how to do that deliberately.

But that was just about to change—a big way.

Emptiness equals happiness. There's no meaning in form until we decide to give it any. Staying deliberately in the emptiness of mind, which can be simply achieved by stopping giving meaning to anything we can notice, sense, and perceive, is another direct path to dropping back to our hearts and experiencing the perfection and love we already are. You are not your mind. You are not your thoughts.

You are not your preferences. You are not your past. You are not your circumstances. You are pristine, perfect, shining love. (In the photo with my friend Lorelle, www.LorelleDehnhard.com).

19
THE MEANING OF MEANINGLESSNESS

Any meaning you give to any thing or person or circumstance is mind-created. Every thing, circumstance, or person, however, is in its default state, free of any meaning. In other words, it is completely empty—until you give it a meaning. Or, if you will, your MIND gives it a meaning.

When you are born, NOTHING has meaning. Everything is without a description until somebody tells you what meaning you should see behind that given thing, or person, or place. When you grow older, your personal experiences will reinforce these and add your own, personal meaning.

Let's say that a boy meets a dog for the very first time. As yet, it has NO meaning for him. It just IS. He has no reference for it, no description of it, no experience with it.

So, he stares at the dog, with all his innocence. That's the beauty of the meaninglessness and emptiness; it still allows a lot of innocence, as opposed to the overloaded, scattered mindsets we start having a few years later. And out of curiosity, the boy starts connecting with the dog from his heart (truly authentic curiosity comes from heart, not mind), rather than mind (which is empty and without reference).

People adore children in moments like this—the moments of the first discoveries. That's because the innocence, heart-fullness and absolutely sweet, natural authenticity come through. For a moment, it reminds us of who we truly are (and fortunately, who we can become again). And that's also why moments like that are very PRESENT moments, during which we stop chasing our minds in a never-ending flow of internal noise. We open our curiosity and hearts, just for a moment, waiting to see what will happen next.

Now imagine, that there is a shift in the experience, and the dog BARKS at the child. Next, either: a) the boy thinks that the dog wants to play with him and sees it as a positive event; or b) the boy gets frightened, pulls away, and sees it as a negative event.

But, in essence, nothing happened. The dog still just IS.

But he did something unexpected, so the mind gave a MEANING to it. And after that, this child might become a lifelong lover or hater of dogs.

So, the meaning that was given to the child by his mind just created his life reality.

Read that sentence again.

Of course, there may be different outcomes to this scenario, but you get the basic lesson: the meaning created literally a new reality for this kid for his whole life, or at least a certain part of it. His reality will be either, "dogs are awesome and friendly," or "dogs are unfriendly and can be even dangerous." And that's how we create our realities!

By giving meaning to meaningless stuff.

Because nothing has meaning until your mind gives it some. Then it creates your reality.

Your reality reflects the way you see it, which is defined by the meanings you give to the people, objects, and places in it.

Only you give meaning to things. But the meaning of love cannot be forced. There are probably still too many deeply rooted limiting and contradictory beliefs in your mind. That's why we first need to let go of our mental bubbles, of our limiting beliefs, and then the direct path to realization to that love can be established. Once you are aligned with that source of the love you already are again, it gets much easier to start changing the meanings of so-called "external reality."

So, if you give meaning to the opposite sex that it cannot be trusted, this is how you will keep experiencing your reality of it (despite no empirical evidence that it is ultimately true, and that other people have different perceptions of reality with the opposite sex).

Or, if you give a meaning to flying on an airplane such as, "this is very dangerous," you'll probably never travel far and won't see much of this world, despite the statistical evidence that flying is the safest way to travel (but your reality of it will be very different, due to the meaning you assigned to it).

And if you give a meaning to this world like, "unfriendly and unkind," this is what you will be experiencing and why you will be permanently living in fear and worries.

Now, the whole thing with meanings is, unfortunately, much more complicated and complex, because a lot of meanings were literally "programmed" into us, despite our free will, by the media, our friends and family, propaganda, social norms, etc. For example, after November 2011 there was a lot of deliberate media propaganda against Muslims. Many people started giving them a negative meaning, even though most of them are incredibly peaceful, friendly, and heart-opened people (at least this is my experience and my reality).

Or, consider how commercial ads push the idea that stretch marks are something ugly and unattractive to men, so that many women give them a new meaning. They develop a new insecurity-based reality, despite the fact that most men don't even know or care what stretch marks are (I honestly did not know until today, and I totally don't care.)

You see, how our perception and experience of reality can be easily manipulated?

But that's primarily because we have too much importance, meaning, and attention generated by our minds!

If you could live from your HEART most of the time, the experience and meaning of everything would be completely different. More of the love we already are would be flowing, so everything would be more connected, and we would definitely see this world as a beautiful place, Muslims as lovely people just like any other, and artificial problems in the ads on TV as nonsense created to sell us something. Because the love you already are would rather reflect who you really are, without caring about some stupid stretch marks. That's what it means to create your reality from HEART, through LOVE and the ultimate truth, not through MIND.

> **If you could live from your heart most of the time, the experience and meaning of everything would be completely different.**

What are you without your thoughts? Without your mind? Try to stop your mind and all its descriptions, opinions, preferences, and conclusions. What will remain? Without the mind, you will naturally drop into your heart. Because you are not your mind. You can use your mind wisely, but any intention needs to flow from

your heart first, to be it truly authentic, truly "you." You are love and heart first, mind second. It is very important to detach from the mind and align back to heart. Become the love you already are again. The perfection of your pure heart. And then start taking any action from that alignment, not from the highly programmed and scattered mind, full of crap. The mind needs to be a good servant of the heart. Not the other way around.

And that's why detaching from mind is very important too.

It doesn't mean you can't keep using it, but you need to stop prioritizing it over your heart. This is a challenge because your mind has been perfectly trained to get most of its attention—80 to 90 percent, on a normal day. Thus it will keep fighting to retain that attention with all its will power.

But if you keep prioritizing the mind and letting it be in charge, it will be very hard to live in and from the love you already are.

It must be your heart giving meanings to reality, not your mind. It must be love giving meaning to your reality if you want to experience a kinder, more loving and connected life.

Mind = mostly meaning based on fear and worries.

Heart = mostly meaning based on openness, connection, love, freedom, and self-acceptance.

YOUR CHOICE.

Now, the only question is how we can achieve that.

How can we make our mind emptier and emptier, detach from it more and more, so our heart can take over?

This was the last technique I had to learn.

20

NETTI NETTI

Because the mind problem can never be solved from the mind level, we need to go to some very deep meditations to do that. At Bentinho Massaro's retreat in Baarlo, Lorelle and I found the solution, a meditation called Netti Netti. It helped us find exactly what we were looking for—the answer to how to empty our minds.

In Sanskrit, "neti neti" means "not this, not this." When used as a meditation term, it indicates a pure lack—the result of an empty mind. I found this meditation profoundly powerful. I use it on my live "You Are Love" retreats, and people love it. This meditation is long; sometimes I go with people for over an hour and a half, yet afterwards, most people feel like it lasted only twenty minutes.

So, what is this mind-emptying meditation about? Don't ask.

As with any self-exploration, this only works if you do it with fully opened heart, not with your brain. (Just return to the five heart agreements you made with yourself at the beginning of this book!) It is crucial with meditations to EMPTY, to PURIFY. But some people, afraid to actually get to that state, decide they must "learn more" about the meditation itself. Instead of just starting to practice, to empty their already overloaded minds, they feel the need to study the history of the meditation and compare it with others—they deconstruct it, compartmentalize it, conceptualize it, and do just about anything but PRACTICE IT.

This is just another manner of avoidance, postponement, pretending, and not allowing. It is an ego-driven distraction and a diversion from heart.

There is ZERO benefit in acquiring more "knowledge" about a certain type of meditation. The point is to *surpass* mind, so your true self before/behind mind can be accessed, so it doesn't fill your brain even more.

That's also why so many people do not move in their lives. They stay in the same bubble, just playing a game of "being smarter" in that bubble because now they "understand." It is a bubble of "intellectual understanding," instead of direct experience. But besides filling up the bubble with more crap, nothing else changes.

So, if you truly want to experience the profound impact of the Netti Netti meditation, you need to PRACTICE it. And not think about it or study it.

PRACTICE.

Netti Netti is an advanced meditation, so start when you feel ready, when your heart feels aligned to it. You'll know when you are ready.

This meditation works only if you do it at least for thirty minutes, no less. I personally do it for forty-five to sixty minutes, and on my "You Are Love" retreats, we go even longer.

Because of the length of the meditation, and because it needs experienced guidance, I am not going to relate the entire sequence here, but let you download it for FREE at www.YouAreLoveBook.com/love.

Let everything be exactly as it is.

But, to introduce you to what it is about, here are the basics steps. The order can be changed, and there are variations that I like to use based on the specific energy and needs at my retreats.

1. **Close your eyes and relax.** Take a few deep breaths; inhale and exhale.

2. **Start paying attention to anything that arises in your consciousness.** Thoughts, feelings, body-sensations: just notice anything.

3. **Watch it, without being engaged with anything.** Act as if you were nothing but an observer. Let everything be exactly as it is. Do not try to change it or escape it. Just let everything be EXACTLY as it is (very important!).

4. **Also notice images that pop up in your mind.**

5. **After a few minutes (or sooner, if you feel like it), start giving everything that came to mind away by saying, "I am not this."** If an image arises, say, "I am not this," and watch as it gets softer and softer, until it eventually disappears. If a thought or body sensation or feeling arises, say, "I am not this," and let it again slowly fade out into nothingness, into empty space. Do not push anything, and have a very strong CONVICTION when you are saying, "I am not this." MEAN IT!

6. **After a few minutes, start speeding this process up, so you create a perpetual loop of "not-this*ness*", and keep**

giving away everything that arises. "NOT THIS-NOT THAT!" Keep going until the space inside of your consciousness feels emptier and emptier. You are literally deleting meanings from anything—including the sensation of YOU (which is a good thing, because this is not your TRUE you. It is a mind-created construct formed in your head, based on the personal and biased feedback that others have been providing to you during your entire life.)

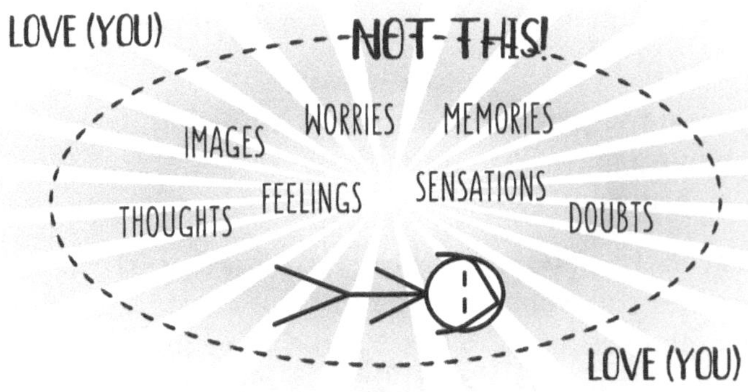

'You Are Love' process STEP #3 - Mindless Love: Whatever arises in your consciousness is not you. Try to disassociate from anything that arises in your consciousness with the Netti Netti meditation and relax into what remains. That's where the peace from mind is found. That's where the love you already are is experienced. If it is not love, it is not you. (Note: You also need to drop your ideas and imagination of what unconditional love is. These are often programmed beliefs and ideas too, including social, cultural, and religious biases, as well as Hollywood romantic movies.)

This meditation can go even further in more advanced versions, but if you start with just this, it is a perfect beginning.

You can practice this for months and months and start having really great results with it.

People at my "You Are Love" retreats are experiencing profound peace, silence, stillness, and relief during this meditation. They all of a sudden feel lighter, free of old worries, fears, and insecurities. Even people experienced in meditation often say that this was the deepest they ever went.

So, download the FREE guided version and try it yourself. You'll probably need several sessions to overcome your internal noise and experience a new level of bliss. But some of the peace and easiness will probably surface during your first attempt. You will already be moving forward. The great thing about this meditation is that it opens you to two possible ways to return to the love you already are, simultaneously:

First, if you keep practicing, it will keep emptying your mind to the point that a lot of meanings will disappear. Then, if you are fortunate, the love you already are will start shining through you naturally, bit by bit, more and more.

And second, even if this does not happen, you still did something incredible—you emptied your consciousness of as many meanings as possible. So, now you have a clean space, a clean "canvas" on which you can start painting whatever you want. You can start increasing your thoughts and actions in line with the love you already are because now you have a new, huge SPACE for it. And this will also be the new content your reality will start being filled with; this will be your new meaning! Just imagine how amazing it will be, exchanging all that crap with LOVE!

At my retreats, we usually do a lot of emptying together on the first day, and then allowance of unconditional love on the second day. So, when the retreat is over, many people feel filled with love, because they cleared a SPACE for it first!

You see, whichever of the three techniques presented in this part of the book you choose, they all are mainly about emptying. It is incredibly freeing to open up a new space for love. And, when you can focus on that, your mind will stop constantly getting more meaning over the heart. With a continuous emptying of mind, the healthy balance will be restored again, and the heart will start being opened more than ever before.

Detach from your mind. You are not it, either. Yes, you still can keep using it (and you have to), but stop prioritizing it.

You are not your mind.

You are love.

21

FROM LOVE WE LEARN
AND GROW

Before we move to the small surprise I have for you in the next chapter, as an end of this "heavier" part of the book, let me share with you one more very important thing.

A lot of people ask me: what is it like?

What is it like going through an enormous transformation towards the love you already are? What is it like to keep purifying more and more, until the love you already are is the main force in your life? What is it like to realize clearly how we have been living with the superficial dogma, "from pain and struggle we grow"? (Hm. Why do you think that we struggle and live in pain for so long with a belief like this?)

You can begin to answer such questions when you understand that it is not pain and struggle from which we prosper. It is LOVE from which we learn and grow. There is a big difference in growing in our lives from struggle and from love.

This alone should give you an enormous incentive to really start working on your own realization of the love you already are. Just imagine how different your life can and will be when love becomes the main force and principle in your life, instead of endless struggle and pain. We take for granted that we must all go through this because we see it all around us. That is because we have attached that meaning to growth and wisdom.

You can be forgiven for mistaking this condition as unavoidable. Even if you have already started building maximum intention, desire, and patience for the realization of the love you already are today, you may still experience some discomfort. You have already seen me break through my week from hell and other difficult periods. It's true that practicing allowance and acceptance sucks. But it is only for the first a few months until you recognize them as natural and they become effortless.

For too long, we have been trained to keep avoiding acceptance, especially of the things that we don't like and don't prefer. So acceptance is a profound shift in our lives. It is pretty rough at the very beginning when we realize that acceptance cannot be selective. It must be absolutely unconditional. We have to be open to taking in everything, and that can be, briefly, painful, challenging, and confusing. I once heard that it feels like "reverse birth"—as though you were giving birth backwards: you would have to suck everything in.

But do not get discouraged by this phase. You already know from this book what my challenges, feelings, and experiences were. Despite their intensity, I am still here, still living, and I am more connected and heart-centered than ever. My life has changed significantly during the last few years.

The journey will be a bit different for everybody. In my case, it goes in stages. Usually, first you have occasional, random, unexpected blasts or glimpses here and there, and you almost don't give it any attention or meaning, or just very little. For too long, we have been trained to focus mainly on our hardship and suffering. So at first, you'll probably be preoccupied with all the bad crap coming out during your first 'releasing' with the techniques I shared previously. That's how the majority of us operate: we first gravitate towards the painful, and ignore the amazing behind it. And that is okay, it is also part of the purification process.

But if you keep going, these random and sudden blasts will be more and more frequent, deeper, and more intense. They still might be confusing sometimes, or you still might lend them no significance or meaning (yes, human ignorance, when it comes to hearts and love, is often staggeringly hilarious.) You will also notice some changes in your relationships, and possibly, more people, mainly the opposite sex, will seem to be attracted to you.

BUT DO NOT STOP HERE.

Keep going, whatever happens.

You need to finish this journey, get back to the love you already are, and open your heart as much as possible, permanently, while drawing from the source of the love you already are very carefully.

If you'll keep going with letting go, and achieve deeper and deeper levels of acceptance and allowance, the feeling of love and ease and connectedness and intimacy will be more and more present, at any time, at any place, without anybody doing anything. It will take some time to get used to it and to adapt, but the feeling will GROW. Your life will very likely start blooming, **You will shine again.**

after you purify it of all that crap that doesn't even belong to you and does not define who you truly are. You will shine again. You will rediscover your inner light and will start living from it again.

But you still need to keep going with purification. There are a lot of limiting layers to break through. With the source of the love you already are, there will also be a lot of new empowerment flowing into you, but only if you keep purifying. Fortunately, at this stage, it is usually very simple to keep committed to the purification techniques and enjoy them every day.

At certain times, you might also feel vulnerable. That is okay, too; this happens when your heart is suddenly really opened. Accept and allow it. The vulnerability and associated pain will be strong initially, but through time, and I am talking months, it will be weaker and weaker. It will literally feel like cleaning up your emotional energy and emotional consciousness. It will not bother you after a few months. It just needs time. Do not avoid anything!

If you keep going, you'll soon realize that there is a mysterious beauty inside vulnerability, and it is so strong and powerful that you can never be vulnerable anymore again. It is another paradox—but the deeper vulnerability you allow, and the more of it you accept, the faster you will feel truly invincible. Once you fully accept your vulnerability, almost magically, people will not be able to hurt you anymore. In many cases, because of that, they'll even stop trying. I found great power, innocence, strength, beauty, love, and connectedness in full acceptance of vulnerability. In fact, now I love it. Sometimes I wish I felt vulnerable all the time. There is some indescribable mystery and very deep innocence and authenticity in it. Perhaps one day, I will, who knows. You never know where this journey will take you next.

You never know where this journey will take you next.

Of course, with all the interior acceptance and honest, authentic, and vulnerable self-love you start experiencing, your outer life will start changing too. At first, you will stand out a bit. Most people in today's society, especially in the West, live with closed hearts. Disconnection, trouble communicating with each other, and fear of intimacy prevail. Most people fear love. Now, you will start getting back all that you have lost over the years. It will be a newly found treasure—your authentic YOU. You will feel like shouting about love to the world, but it is likely that nobody will be listening to you. Those close to you might not want to join your quest to your newly opened, warm, loving, and welcoming heart.

For some time, you might feel alone. It's lonely, wanting to share this amazing love when there are no receivers. People will still seem to prefer being closed in their bubbles, preferring "safety," ignorance, and disconnection instead of love. That is okay too. It took me some time to figure this out, but it is part of the ACCEPTANCE!

It is just a sign you need to keep accepting and allowing.

Keep going with DEEP acceptance, including the pain of being full of love but having it nowhere to express it. Don't worry. The connection with the love you are will be deepening even more, and you will start to glimpse true ONENESS. That is really the next level, another amazing, profound experience of life and being.

And that turning point can start bringing some REALLY significant changes in your life. Your true life purpose can start emerging, you can become a powerful manifestor of your reality, and you will definitely start experiencing a new level of connection with people.

At that point of acceptance, you will literally start loving and hugging the entire world, and you will have transcended your entire life into a blast of excitement, connection, love, intimacy, joy, and meaningfulness. There still will be challenges, but there will be one HUGE shift: You will start realizing that the old "from pain, we learn and grow" theme doesn't apply to you anymore. You will not know hardship as you might have known it before. Instead, your new reality will be "from LOVE we learn and grow."

And that will become your new mantra, life force, and organizing principle of your life. From love, we learn and grow. Open up to it and allow it fully!

22
THE RECONNECT MEDITATION

I know this part of the book required a lot from you. Purification is not easy after we have become too full of things that don't define who we truly are. So, it requires certain measures to get things back to the natural state. But believe me, it is all worth it. Just go full in. As your reward, I would like to finish Part Two on a slightly softer note, to give you something nice and easy, which you will probably love.

I have a very special meditation for you. It is one of the most beautiful and gentle meditations I have experienced during more than ten years of being a daily meditation practitioner. It is not as direct as Netti Netti, but it is beautiful, and it brings some very pleasant and immediate results too.

The author of this meditation is my friend Rion Kati, from whom I learned a tremendous amount about living a purpose-aligned life and about ALLOWANCE. Rion is a founder of a technique called Natural Grounding, which is a form of allowance practice based on connecting to music and music video performance.

In 2016, I met with Rion in Los Angeles together with a few other guys, and we spent several nights experiencing deep connection through allowance—with the help of Rion's Natural Grounding technique and guidance. We played highly emotional music videos and let ourselves surrender to their energy.

For example, we played the "Unconditional" music video from Katy Perry, in order to give ourselves up to the field of the energy and vibration of unconditional love. This music video took the place of a permission slip and became a jumping-off point for allowing unconditional love to flow.

During that week, with Rion's leadership, we did extensive work on allowance and experienced new depths of unconditional connections on many levels.

How much unconditional allowance are you willing to accept in your life? The more you allow allowance of unconditional love to flow, the more it will. But without allowance, it can't even start.

> **How much unconditional allowance are you willing to accept in your life?**

Use whatever permission slip serves you to build a massive allowance. This trigger toward massive allowance of the unlimited power of your true, highest self can be found in music videos and other incentives. Whatever works for you, use it. The method of using music videos as "permission-slips" was developed and revolutionized by my friend Rion Kati (on the right side on the photo). He called that process "Natural Grounding" and had some massive breakthroughs, thanks to it. That's because music settles closer to heart than to mind. It helps us connect to our higher selves faster, and with less thinking, conceptualization, and rationalization.

Here is the gift meditation, courtesy of Rion. Before you start reading it, get back to your five Heart Agreements. You have to go through this meditation with your heart as open as possible. Then just read the text slowly, at your own pace, and let your heart be impacted and cleansed by its beautiful words.

Also, you can download a lovely, recorded mp3 version in the FREE bonuses at <u>www.YouAreLoveBook.com/love</u>. Once you listen to it, you will fall in love with it. You'll want to have it in your mobile phone all the time. So just get it, and start using it today. It really is beautiful. I have listened to this meditation at least two hundred times already.

So, open your heart and enjoy!

Cleansing Meditation by Rion Kati (published with his generous approval):

Relax into a state of open readiness for this private meditation. In this heart-connected open space, you are now ready for this special experience. There is no one here to judge you. Allow the frequency of your heart to rise and heal as best it can throughout. Do not be afraid of it or the power of getting emotional. For love heals all. It is a source of strength, power, and healing.

Now visualize yourself on a majestic grasslands plain in South Africa, on a beautiful springbok morning, to speak to your heart, for something new to unfold, as you make space by clearing out the clutter in your heart. Now is the time to be vulnerable and open, like a child. Like you are waiting in anticipation of something big in another part of you, from a great rain, shine, perhaps an awakening or a great rite of passage is evident, and it is time. Don't resist whatever emotions come out. Let them flow, and even flood in this healing meditation.

Heart is Universal emotional consciousness, and higher frequencies of it are pure love and experiential happiness. And, oh, how you value your heart, and how, as alive, you value freedom and you deserve freedom, which is through expression. And if you have not expressed, you have suppressed. Thus, you have often denied, or hidden your heart. You have been suppressing some things for far too long, and this has caused all kinds of energy blocks, stress, stored up inside of your heart and chakras. As you open yourself up to the deep power of higher heart consciousness, you allow yourself to be affected by the lower resonance. This voice, and the voice of Africa, the cry of freedom for all people, freedom from struggle, freedom from all judgment, you love and accept yourself for who you are.

Go with it, and as you let a higher emotional frequency shake the mud and crust off of your core, you further allow your own heart to start resonating with it. With power, beauty, and the unconditional love itself, you allow the darkness and storm to happen, for you know it is a healing storm, and there will be a calm after the storm.

Allow the rains to come and wash away, sacrificing your clutter so that you can be free now. Do not be afraid, and instead of resisting the great thunderstorm, you allow it to happen and take over you, as you connect with higher unconditional love itself. Could it be too beautiful? Could you be worthy of freedom? Is it too good for you? Do you accept yourself for who you are? You forgive yourself. Could that beauty really exist in your heart?

As you resonate with it, you let your state flow more. You hear the voice of the African plains in the wind, of free nature. This brings healing power from higher heart consciousness to you, your heart wants to speak and be free. You are giving it a voice now to heal itself. Bask in this new territory, on this African plain. The voice of Africa is the voice of all heart here and now, from spirit, raw, all the past trials and tribulations have been there to form and forge your character, throughout all of the pressure, you have always been a diamond in the rough. Allow the rains to wash the mud off of your diamond, and your inner shining brilliance for you.

Let it all go out into the wild to be in a state of pure heart and freedom, a new experience of self. Stop resisting what is. You received the storm that wants to cleanse you, so you can be a shining example and expression of your inner beauty, and more life to awe. Yes, let it rain. Express, don't suppress, and submissively let go to a power greater than yourself. You are forgiven and you are loved. You resonate Universal love and compassion in a higher state of awareness. Let the act of submission itself physically overwhelm you. In total humility, you may fall on the floor, weeping. You ARE loved.

This power to heal yourself can also heal others, many
others, and brings great direct wellness into your life. Love
is ever-present, accept it. Now, give thanks to Mother Africa
from your heart, as you dissolve from the vista into the present
moment here and now, and enter a more normal state of consciousness, allowing your heart to just be, more openly expressive
in the now. You value heart and carry this more open, dynamic,
expressive, healed and healing consciousness out into your world,
in greater vitality, health, and wellness, and you give thanks for
this heart awakening and healing meditation.

PART II: QUESTIONS & ANSWERS

Q: *How do acceptance and letting go work together?*

We cannot let go of what we don't accept first. If we don't accept it, it means it is still an attachment, we prefer holding onto (otherwise we would accept it and let it be "free," as it is already). That's why we have to embrace all the emotions in the Letting-Go Process first. Once accepted, they are ours to let go of.

Sometimes, the acceptance and the letting go happens at the same time. Again, this is quite often the case with the Letting-Go Process, but it also happens during emotional purification. But we can never purify without acceptance. This is always the very first step. To accept EXACTLY where we are. And again, not PRETENDING we are accepting, but accepting it fully. Accept things just as they are, without trying to escape or modify them.

This is what I was doing during the emotional purification experiment. Remember? Yes, it is uncomfortable for a short time, because we have been avoiding and pretending for too long. But it is worth the effort. The love we already are can never flow until we let go of the attachments that don't define who we truly are. These attachments can never be let go of, and often not even recognized, without full acceptance.

So, the point is to stop trying to get SOMEWHERE— including with this book. Notice how you might be reading it just to try to get to a certain point or pull something useful from it. That means you have still not accepted where you are NOW. And without that, letting go is not possible.

Fortunately, all the techniques explained in this part of the book can help you with that, and do so pretty quickly.

Q: *I have realized I am too attached to opinions others have about me. How can I let go of them?*

First of all, congratulations! It takes time, dedication, courage, and a very high level of self-honesty for most people admit this.

This is also what I often point to in this book as "social validation." Without realizing it, we spend most of our days trying to do things to look good in the eyes of others. This activity turns us into validation addicts. We are not able to positively validate ourselves (as we were not trained to do so; quite the opposite), so we constantly run our lives to make sure we are permanently seen by others as a good person, good mother, the right team member, the right employee, etc. Most of our actions in our lives are motivated by getting some kind of approval, or recognition, or positive validation, so we can finally give ourselves permission to feel good, at least for a while. And even if you think you *can* validate yourself positively, you are still subconsciously seeking external confirmation of that positive self-validation. If it doesn't come, you begin to doubt yourself. So, it is again a validation addiction, just a different kind, a bit more sophisticated.

And most of that can be summarized as "being too dependent on what people think about me" (which again is nothing more than validation addiction). This is part of heavy social programming (we all were programmed like this, including me) and it doesn't allow us to express ourselves truly, freely, authentically, and naturally.

That's why we all need to realize the source of the love we already are. Our main intent is to realize that we already are perfect, that everything is already within us. We have the power to feel 100 percent great, awesome, happy, and loved—highly aligned—despite any opinion of other programmed validation seekers.

So, keep this in your consciousness: your intent to be liberated from this attachment and addiction. Keep practicing all the techniques from this part of the book, so you can start realizing the source of the love you already are and start living from this amazing source, instead of from external validations and opinions.

Liberate yourself from the assumptions you've made about yourself, especially those based on the highly personal opinion that others have about you. Don't forget, you are nothing but love. So be that love, live that love, and stop paying any attention to all that other validation seekers around you. Become a full-hearted inspiration and motivation for them, bring them to your heart, overwhelm them with the presence of the love you are. This will help you stop wanting or needing anything *from them*, especially validations, opinions, or assessments. And stop demanding the same from yourself, as well!

Q: *Is my lifelong attempt to get recognition from my parents an attachment I should let go of too?*

Absolutely! And one you should let go of as soon as possible. Remember my story about the boy and the dog? If no one told that child that dogs are dangerous, he might accept the playful intention of a bark. How are your parents different than other people?

Like most individuals, they are probably not aligned to the love they already are. They, too, probably lived most of their lives in validation addiction. So, why should you try to direct your life in the way that makes THEM happy, and get a bit of recognition from them?

Love them! But let go of all that other stuff. It is nonsense that I had to deal with in the past too. Guilt and shame about what we think we are supposed to do get in the way of our true selves.

All that matters is to align back to the love you already are, and then start living from that source. Let go of the need to prove something to someone, to get any kind of recognition from anyone, or to please someone—even your parents. That's all just crap costing you too much of energy and happiness. Recognition is not an enduring reward, just a few seconds of a good, pleasant feeling. Let go of that, so the true and authentic peace, happiness, and joy can start shining through you.

PART III

LIVE & GIVE

The greatest receiver of love is the one who's constantly giving it, without expecting anything in return.

23

THE TREMENDOUS POWER OF GIVING LOVE

Congratulations, you made it to the final part of this book. I am very proud of you. The love you already are must be calling you; otherwise, you wouldn't have made it so far! You're awesome.

So, now let's talk about living from love and giving love. I'd like to start by sharing my own experience first.

When I was writing this book, I felt like giving a lot of love. My main intention from the beginning was to spread more love, through helping amazing people like you realize how much love you truly are, and that you CAN live from this most of the time, rather from fears, worries, and insecurities.

And of course, this act of giving love felt INCREDIBLE.

Because the more love you give, the more it flows through you. It doesn't matter what the form of giving is.

As I wrote, I had moments when I literally felt like I was living in a parallel reality. I would sit in a café, typing away, and on some occasionsm I felt such intense blasts of bliss, beauty, and heart-openness that I thought everyone must notice. I felt such an intimacy with the world around me that I thought I might scare the people seated nearby! :-)

Instead, I attracted them. I met some amazing people while spending endless hours in different cafés. I especially remember one: an older Spanish lady approached me one day, and we had a very nice, connected, heart-opened chat. When I was about to leave for an appointment, she started singing for me, in Spanish, in front of everyone in the cafeteria! As you can imagine, I was truly touched. What a gracious person she was. I so appreciated her displaying the grace we all possess, which so many people keep inside.

On another day, I was writing about dancers (a story for another book) when, all of sudden, a former ballet dancer started chatting with me. When she learned what I was writing, she shared details about her years as a dancer, things that gave me deeper insight into that life. I was truly amazed and, again, touched by all of her generous storytelling. It was another spontaneous, authentic, heart-opened, connected conversation. And I enjoyed quite a few more during the writing of this book.

Because I was aligned with the source of the love I am, and because I opened myself to giving it to others, amazing things happened all the time. Besides the human connections, I also very easily put together the capital needed to launch this book and get it out in the world. It was a substantial sum. Since I began my journey, my life took a turn toward the magical and exciting.

On top of those fortuitous events, while making sure to write this book only from highly aligned states, I learned so much more about trusting and having faith. There were days when I had no idea what I should write about. Yet, I was confident that the right words would emerge as soon as I opened my laptop. And they always did.

Sometimes, I felt like I didn't want to write, so I didn't. I took the week off. And after that week, I felt so charged that I wrote more in one day than I normally would in a whole week!

All the time, whatever I felt inspired to do next, I maintained a perfect trust that it would be the right step, without planning too far ahead. My intuition-based actions would not make much sense for the average mind, trained to think linearly and be preoccupied by absolutely everything. But it felt easy for me to trust that intuition, as it felt aligned and connected to heart. I could sense that I would naturally do the right thing. It felt great!

That's another amazing thing about living from the love you already are. With an opened heart, all of sudden, you trust. You have faith. You love your intuition, trust it 100 percent, don't question it, and then watch events unfold, just right, each time. Because true, authentic intuition comes from heart, not from mind! We have only been trained to believe our minds more than intuition, so it's a simple equation to reverse and regain that trust in our internal wisdom.

With an opened heart, all of sudden, you trust. You have faith.

Whatever involves an opened heart is always so much more powerful and prolific than the limitations placed by our minds.

So the more I put trust and faith and alignment into writing this book, the more I was literally channeling it, instead of writing it. The source of the love we already are was feeding me with inspiration all the time, effortlessly, gently, and joyfully! The more I felt I was channeling the TRUTH about what we are (pristine love), the more I felt that source of love flowing through me, on deeper, or newer, or as-yet undiscovered levels.

So my only goal during the writing of this book was to remain in that state of faith and ALLOWANCE, preserving the intention of GIVING that love and making sure I was in full alignment whenever typing on the keyboard. If I had days when the love we already are was not flowing (which is normal, as it usually means you still have some lessons to learn or more crap to let go of), I did not write, because the content of this book would not be true—it would be made up by mind instead of channeled from heart.

As great a challenge and adventure writing this book was, each day I was realizing more and more the tremendous power of giving love. The clearer and more unselfish my intentions were, the easier everything FLOWED, the more joy and excitement I experienced, the more connected I felt to everything (and especially myself), the more I felt like being in amazing love—without anybody doing anything.

I simply learned that giving unconditional love is incredibly joyful and rewarding.

But the trick is that, first, love truly needs to be unconditional (no expectations, no waiting if/when something happens, no being attached to any results, yet staying in an openness of full allowance of anything). Second, you need to come from the place of giving because you already have realized the amazing source of the love you already are (as opposed to taking any action for more validation, or for compensation of personal wants and needs of any kind). And third, you need to balance love with a kind of wisdom.

Especially, the last one is important, because it is quite easy to become a "giver" just for the sake of others seeing you as "love" and a "giver." But, isn't that just another form of seeking validation? You shouldn't need others to "confirm" you are a giver and a loving person. This is still wanting something from others, and not truly giving unconditionally. In other words, giving love with wisdom means knowing already where you are coming FROM (from the source of the pristine love you already are) instead of where you want to gravitate toward. Perhaps this is connected to intuition, which we can access once our hearts are open.

But with more and more of the love you already are flowing through you, this will become more and more effortless, automatic, and joyful. It will also tremendously fast-track a deeper realization of your infinite perfection.

Because it is something I would love you to start experiencing as soon as possible (even now!), the last part of this book will be about five simple ways you can give LOADS of unconditional love to others, without sacrificing anything, while being deeply connected to the love you already are. If you start practicing them, I promise you will start seeing some amazing changes in your life very fast.

So, get back to the agreements you made with yourself at the beginning of this book. Open your heart as much as possible again, and set out to practice the five incredibly powerful ways to give loads of unconditional love to others and thus hasten the realization of the perfection and love you already are.

24

GIVING SILENCE AND STILLNESS

Do you consider yourself an introvert or an extrovert?

If your answer is "none of that, I consider myself to be nothing by pure love," then, congratulations. You've been paying attention.

But before you picked up this book, you probably had some idea about your mannerisms. In general, people labeled "introverts" tend to prefer remaining in silence, and "extroverts" like talking a lot. If you do both, then an ultra-smart society would have a label for you too— an "introvert-extrovert"! :-)

I used to consider myself an extrovert for a long time. I am a highly communicative person, and being quiet used to be hard for me. But not surprisingly, this started changing, the more I became connected to my heart.

How's that?

Think about it. In the most beautiful moments of your life, when you felt perfect peace and harmony, when you felt loved and loving, receiving and giving, truly connected to the source of the love you already are—how many words were spoken? Did you feel the need to talk? Probably not at all.

The truth is that the most beautiful moments in life usually pass in *silence!*

You probably don't talk much while watching a dazzling sunset on the horizon. You don't talk much while looking deeply and lovingly into the eyes of another person (or at least I hope you don't). You probably don't feel like having a long conversation when your kids are hugging you and overwhelming you with love.

The best moments of life often happen in silence because our heart simply doesn't need words! It has its own language. You can perfectly connect with people without a single word, often on deeper and truer levels than through words.

Yet, we still love talking too much!

We are too attached to talking. Too eager to be always heard and recognized through what we say out loud. (Yes, another validation addiction!)

We talk, instead of quietly radiating the love we already are and enjoying the presence of it. But silence can be extremely powerful.

Healing.

But silence can be extremely powerful.

Cleansing.

Thus, you can give so much love if you just create a container of love, invite other people into it, and then stay completely silent. Focus on your love-presence, instead of on words and your eagerness to be seen and heard.

Seriously!

You'll be surprised how easy it is to become a giver when you let your heart do all the "speaking," instead of using mind-created words. People will notice, believe me; yet you won't need their validation any more.

There is also a profound reason why silence is powerful. Talkativeness is always related to our minds and egos, not our hearts. Too much talking is generally an effort to push OUR own agenda and OUR own opinions on others. That is a means of looking for validation and seeking what we can get OUT of the situation, instead of staying in the presence of the love we already are, which doesn't need any external validation. It is absolutely self-fulfilling!

You might disagree with that, but once you start being more observant and aware of the difference between speaking and being silent, especially in situations where you'd normally talk a lot, you will gain new insights and revelations about yourself. And I don't mean this in a judgmental way; I am just suggesting what might be better for your heart now and then. Simply said, silence is an environment in which connection and love grow faster.

In silence, we are forced to calm down our mind, and as a result, it has much less to follow and react to. Thus, mind gets out of its regular job, and we naturally drop from mind into our hearts. Then, heart will start opening more and more, and unifying everything and everyone on a more authentic level— with less ego involved.

In silence, we become truly observant, instead of highly igno-rant. And these are the best moments in which to increase our awareness that our old beliefs and the crap we carry around don't serve us anymore. Their futility will be revealed in silence—and then we can let them go, effortlessly, with a smile on our faces.

In fact, if you manage to reduce your speech by 25 percent during your usual day, the chances are, you will be immediately 25 percent happier.

Just try it out! At least for one week.

Silence will also allow emotions to flow more naturally, because you will not be trying to push them away or cover them up with another activity, like speaking. They will have more chances to be exactly what they are, and that means more nat-ural ALLOWANCE in your life, without any special effort! In fact, you will be doing LESS, so you will also have spare energy.

You've probably heard of special "silent" retreats, and many people who experience them have completely changed their lives. I know that very well from a brother of mine, who once spent an entire week in a dark room, in complete silence. When he went back to "normal life," everything started changing quickly. He almost instantly found the love of his life (they have a beautiful girl together now,) his higher purpose manifested absolutely effortlessly, and he got a few amazing jobs that he loved and which allowed him to contribute to human welfare. In that week of complete silence, his mind could finally be quiet, and his heart finally got the chance to take over the words.

Once you start connecting to the love you already are, you will come to see words as less crucial. You will start experienc-ing and valuing a different way of communicating with others, on different levels which are much warmer, deeper, and less ego-driven. When you use a heart-based communication, you will start naturally and effortlessly attracting people with opened hearts too. So, your entire life will start evolving, all because of less talk and more stillness and silence, so your heart gets a chance to speak too.

Since love started flowing through me, I appreciate staying silent in moments when everybody expects to talk. I attend social gatherings and events where I can stay completely quiet for ten, twenty, thirty minutes, while everybody else can't stop talking for a single second. This silence and stillness allows me to connect with others on a different level (most people will never notice directly, but they will sense it intuitively.) It allows me to be tremendously PRESENT.

Having a real, authentic presence is a beautiful, unconditional way of living. Very few people can do something as simple as that—give an unconditional silence. You remain silent and focus not on words, but on filling your being with the love you already are—without expecting or desiring any validation for that. If you manage to stay silent, still, and highly present, without any need to be engaged in anything or wanting anything, you will give A LOT of love. And you will experience a lot of love, too, along with a peace and calmness.

Talking is overrated; silence and heart are underrated.

When you give unconditional love in the least noticeable way like this, you will realize infinite depth and connection to the love you already are.

Talking is overrated; silence and heart are underrated.

In general, we talk way too much and love way too little! So, let's start changing it.

25

GIVING OTHERS THE OPPORTUNITY TO GIVE

During last few years, I have realized that the biggest disease of this planet is not cancer, or HIV, or Alzheimer's disease, but rather something much simpler:

The sense that we do not deserve unconditional love.

This condition is common. It leaves us feeling that we are not worthy of recognition. Kindness. Gentleness. Appreciation. Nurturement. Attention. Hugs. Love. More love. We don't hurt only ourselves. Because of our belief that we are not worthy, we become astonishingly horrible *receivers!* Therefore, we are depriving other people of the opportunity to GIVE.

It is not always that people don't *want* to give anything unconditionally.

NO!

It is that we are too closed to receiving, as a result of our rooted, often subconscious beliefs that we are not worthy—especially when it comes to unconditional giving.

We say we want unconditional love. But we are too closed for it. We don't feel we are fully and unconditionally worthy of that. We don't believe in unconditional love. So, we prefer having our hearts fully closed. Thus, there are few love receivers in this world. So, make a change. Give away your (self)limiting beliefs. Just open up to receiving unconditional love—but totally unconditionally. Drop your shields. Open your heart. Let go. Surrender. Be the love you already are.

**Drop your shields.
Open your heart.**

We even perceive people who want to give unconditionally as suspicious! That is how closed and ignorant and locked in our unworthiness belief we have become. Of course, that is mostly due to heavy social programming that teaches us, "Don't trust anybody," "Nothing is free," and "Don't open up to other people too easily."

How far do you think you can get when it comes to unconditional receiving, including unconditional love, when you stubbornly hold onto such assumptions, simply because the vast majority seems to be holding the same beliefs? (Note: you just got another idea of what you should let go of.) By holding yourself back, by staying in the role of unworthy "victim," you also deprive other people of the beautiful experience of GIVING.

If there are no receivers, the givers have nobody to give to.

I know people who want to give all the love of the Universe, but they cannot find willing receivers. So, another amazing gift you can give to other people, out of the love you already are, is the opportunity to GIVE. Give them the chance to experience its rewards, so they can keep opening and become purer, heart-connected givers.

Let me again share a short story, about how I learned for the very first time about the gift of giving others the opportunity to give, many years ago.

Over the years, I visited three different retreats in Holland that were highly focused on some serious, deep inner work. Yes, feeling unworthy was one of the key themes of way too many people at all of them. The first two retreats were given by international bestselling author Brandon Bays, the third one by Benthino Massaro, who introduced me to the Netti Netti meditation.

All these events had something in common: the actual work done during them resulted in pretty fast and deep heart openness. Once this happened, a lot of people started expressing authentic love, naturally and spontaneously.

I still remember that the first time, it felt totally WEIRD to me.

It was at the Brandon Bay's two-day retreat called "The Journey." The first day, we did a lot of heavy work on releasing and letting go of old, unnecessary crap. It was similar to my letting-go technique, but I found it longer, difficult, and not as direct to practice. That just made all of us work harder.

But on day two, after the majority of the crap was gone, everything started changing tremendously: people were shining, smiling, they were very warm, connected—quite the opposite of what a typical person experiences on most days.

Of course, that time, my brain was still wired to beliefs like "for love, we have to fight," "no pain, no gain," "there is no free lunch," and "if people are nice to you, they definitely want something from you."

So it felt pretty uncomfortable in a group of people who were suddenly radiating a lot of love, while my own body seemed to be shut down to any *receiving*. There was no trust toward this new experience, nor toward the people daring to express love so nakedly and shamelessly (yes, the heavy social, cultural, and religious conditioning with all those "shoulds" and "shouldn'ts" allows us, in fact, to express very little of the amazing love we all already are—express our true, authentic nature).

I thought there must have been something wrong, either with THEM or ME. Because I used to be very ignorant and arrogant, I chose to believe that it was THEM.

But this belief didn't last long.

After the second day of the retreat, the last mutual breakfast for all the attendees was set, and it happened that I ended up at the same table with probably the six most shining people out of two hundred attending the retreat. Of course, I felt even more uncomfortable, and I blamed all of them for being even weirder than the rest. I remained locked in my closed-ness, ignorance, and arrogance, and I was even enjoying those negative qualities.

As the breakfast continued, though, I saw another person sit down at a nearby table. I had encountered her on the previous days of the retreat; she had described herself as the busy mother of five kids, and she looked the part.

But that particular morning, I did not recognize her right away: she was incredibly shining. She looked as though the previous stress and hardship that had been so visible in her demeanor were completely gone. She looked fifteen years younger. I was shocked to learn that she was actually fifteen years older *than me* at the time!

When I finally identified her, I couldn't believe the obvious difference that I could see in her. This truth caused me to lose my ignorance, closed-ness, and arrogance for a moment. I told her that she looked like she was completely reborn—and this time, as a true Greek goddess.

She turned to me, with a full, kind, gentle smile, and released an enormous amount of the newly found (self)love toward me. It was an indescribable combination of mother's love, nurturing love, appreciating love, very pure feminine love (which is extremely healing) and enormous universal love, all in "one package". And it all came from a pure presence of GIVING.

I was totally NOT ready for that, which may have been a good thing. In my disbelief and shock at the enormous change in this woman, I forgot to control my closed-ness, ignorance, and arrogance, and I suddenly opened to her love.

I **_RECEIVED_** IT ALL.

Normally, this would not happen. I would shy away from receiving, especially THAT vast amount of love. I would prefer to stay ignorant and fully "protecting" my heart, out of the fear of expressing any sign of vulnerability or authenticity—exactly what so many people try to do most of their lives.

But this time I forgot to keep my shield up, and fully unprotected, I received all that love. This robbed me of my usual impulse to categorize and describe what was happening. I was out of words for the rest of the breakfast, still overwhelmed by the experience.

But a more interesting part came next.

When the breakfast was over, I regained my senses. Yet, I still felt deeply touched and enormously grateful. So, I decided to share my whole experience with that mother of five. I approached her and told her openly about what had just happened to me and how grateful I was for that. She listened carefully, then smiled again, gave me a loving hug, and said:

"Thank you too! It felt so good to have somebody who was willing to receive that! It is sometimes very hard to GIVE a bit of unconditional love. I could GIVE, and it felt amazing too."

And that was a big moment for me. With it came a huge revelation:

Giving love means not always being just the giver, but also being the passionate RECEIVER. The more you give people

Giving love means not always being just the giver, but also being the passionate RECEIVER.

the opportunity to express their best and highest potential, like being an unconditional giver, the more love you are giving.

So, stop being selfish. Stop playing that heart-closed role of unworthy victim. We are all ABSOLUTELY worthy of ANY kind of love, all the time—unless we stubbornly insist on the opposite.

Open your heart and give people a chance to give too.

And receive it all, UNCONDITIONALLY.

Let the giver go through that beautiful experience of unconditionally giving as fully as he or she can. Your reception is also a form of giving unconditional love.

26

SEEING OTHERS AS THE HIGHEST POTENTIAL OF LOVE

A few years ago, I co-owned the biggest and the most successful trading school in the Czech Republic, my country of origin. During ten years of growing and nurturing that school with my former business partner, we had literally thousands of people coming through our live seminars.

But what was really surprising to me was that many people attended REPEATEDLY. Even to my most expensive, VIP trading seminars, people came three or even four times, and were willing to pay what, in the Czech Republic, was a steep price, again and again. At first, I didn't understand why it was happening. I thought it must have been because I was doing a poor job—that people didn't understand well enough what I was teaching and, thus, returned to the seminars to gain clarity.

So, I started improving the seminars, simplifying the content, and adding extra, after-the-seminar support. But even with all that, nothing changed; people still came back multiple times!

Of course, from a business perspective, it was great. But from a human perspective, I didn't feel like charging people repeatedly if they could not get what I taught them the first time. I had a lot of inner conflicts because of that, so one day, during another live seminar in Prague, I finally decided to ASK. To learn the exact reason why so many people were paying again and again for the same course.

I was unprepared for the answer I got:

They said that they returned because they felt super encouraged and super-charged after each seminar, because of my energy! Even students who already were highly successful traders, even better than me, were coming to my live events to experience that.

It was the very first time I learned that I had some "energy" that people seemed to be craving, more than the content itself (which I thought to be much more valuable). Because I am curious and always want to learn as much as possible, I started thinking and meditating how and why this energy had grown in me. I wanted to keep giving more of it to them.

After some time and many meditations, I finally figured out why:

The energy that people were feeling as "encouraging" and "super-charging" was created by my outlook. I SAW people as if they already were SUCCESSFUL traders—and treated them accordingly!

Even if they were complete beginners, in my eyes they were already successful, making a lot of money, and realizing their highest potential. I could always see that in my students, so I treated them with respect, as equals who were easily as successful as, or more successful than, me.

And that made all the difference!

That created the energy that was translated into the "encouragement" and "empowerment" they all needed. That was why my seminars were always packed, while the competition struggled to fill their seats.

So, you see, you can add so MUCH value to other people's lives just by the way you SEE them, or rather, you deliberately DECIDE to see them, despite any personal egoistic opinions or circumstances.

And the same applies for love.

You can give a tremendous amount of unconditional love just by making the deliberate decision to *see* other people as nothing but the infinite potential of love.

Despite what they do.

Or how they act.

Or what they think of you (don't forget, you are not a validation addict anymore!).

At the end of the day, this is where we all are coming from. This is our true nature, our true source of existence. So, why not see people like that already?

UNCONDITIONALLY!

By deliberately seeing in other people this highest TRUTH, you create a new reality around you, a reality filled with the same quality—LOVE. Everybody wins and grows then. People feel great, have more trust in themselves, appreciate themselves more, love themselves more. Then they reflect that back to you.

And you keep growing the love you already are, letting it fill your entire presence and consciousness.

If you really want to push this even further, try for one day to label EVERYTHING around you as LOVE.

Forget any other labels.

Forget all your old habits.

Just see love everywhere, in everyone, and in everything.

So, beginning today, start truly, authentically seeing other people like love too. Or at least, start seeing the potential. And by that, I mean just "seeing." *Not* trying to "navigate" them, direct them or give them "good advice." All these are mostly ego-driven activities. Love doesn't have to do anything more than SEE more love—more of itself. That's how it spreads more of itself. It is the "I" (love) gazing at the same "I" (love) in others. That's how it grows and shares.

Love doesn't have to do anything more than SEE more love—more of itself.

Just try this: no labeling, no thoughts, no judgments.

We all are already love, we are just not awakened to it. That should not stop you from seeing the best in people. I am doing it as I write this book: I see the pure potential of endless love in you. I already love you without knowing you. Because, thanks to my direct encounters with love, I cannot think of you in any other way.

Of course, you will not be able to maintain this view all the time—neither can I. But every second that you are able to step out of your bubble and out of the habit of labeling and judging others, you become a selfless/selfish-less love, looking back at itself. This transforms reality.

If you can't see people as their highest potential love yet, or all the time, don't punish yourself for that. It is totally okay. It takes some practice and patience. And for it to be true, you aren't required to see them like that 24/7. If you can do this at least 10 percent of the time, that will make a difference. So, every second DOES matter. The more you see others like love, the more you will see yourself as love.

We are all part of the same consciousness, coming from the same source of love. Help others to grow into enormous love by seeing them that way, and your reality will start being filled with love, connectedness, kindness, and joy.

27

BEING LOVE-PRESENT

I have a friend with a tremendously high level of sexual presence. You'd think being a "sexual alpha"—radiating so much sexual energy naturally—would be great. But when I spent some time with him, I noticed that most women felt a bit intimidated. In fact, the effect on some was the direct opposite of what you would expect. The tension caused by his sexual expression made them react with harsh judgments, just because they didn't know how to deal with that.

So one day I asked him what he does in cases like that, when he feels people are secretly judging him for his natural attractiveness. His reply really got me. He just calmly said:

I simply add more.

In other words, he simply increases his sexual presence even more—becomes *more* himself.

And it makes sense.

This is the current self-expression he decided to have. This is who he decided to be at this stage of his life. So, if anyone has problems with that, it is up to them to look deeper into their belief system, and find out why they pass judgment against other people's self-expression. Why *they* feel insecure. And then, of course, to let all of that go. It doesn't belong to them.

You should do the same when it comes to love-presence.

That means not being afraid of expressing your own overwhelming love-presence in front of other people, like my first instinct was in the café while writing this book. Fortunately, I decided not to give in to that urge but to continue letting the love flow. You should too—and not to get attention or validation, but to be authentic, because this is who you truly are.

To give love means also not to be afraid of love. So, if it radiates strongly and other people feel intimidated by it—add even more of it! At least you are giving them something to reflect on. Through the strong love-presence of another human being, they can finally start seeing the closed-ness of their hearts.

> **To give love means also not to be afraid of love.**

Of course, this is not pleasant for many people. Fear gets in the way of acceptance. But that is also why they attracted this experience into their lives. Because subconsciously, this is what they want at that given moment. And what their soul is pushing them toward. See the contrast? Finally, a strong will starts them moving in the direction of love, despite—and even because of—the initial discomfort, self-denial, and anxiety they feel in a strong love-presence.

Once you return to the source of the love you already are, you need to be a leading example. Again, not for validation. Not in a pushy, unnatural way. Just a kind, soft, authentic example.

Your love-presence alone can have a significant, positive impact on the lives of others, as long as it is truly authentic and free of any ego or intention to get something out of it.

So, never be afraid to be overwhelmingly love-present.

Do not be afraid to feel the intimate connection with yourself directly in front of others. Screw any social dogmas and social "rules." Be a leading example. Give other people cause for reflection.

Be love to the fullest.

Shine love to the fullest.

Fill all the space around you with it.

It doesn't matter how people react. The majority will not, of course, even notice, because the majority of people have their hearts too closed. But some will feel deeply inspired by it, which is great. Other people will feel triggered by that, which is equally great—and, perhaps you are giving these individuals an even bigger benefit. The reason why people are triggered is that they can face their inner insecurities again and again, until they finally decide to resolve them.

Even when people are confused and don't know how to react, persist in giving more. Do not flinch an inch. Add even more of your true, authentic, unconditional love-presence to their world.

Simply prefer LOVE all the time.

Fill everything with the love you already are.

Give more of it. Absolutely shamelessly.

The more you are aligned to the love you already are, the more you fill your whole presence with it.

28

GIVING THE BEST OF YOURSELF IN THE SIMPLEST WAY POSSIBLE

Let me ask you a dare question:

How intimate can you be with yourself?

Don't necessarily interpret intimacy as sexual. Because that's not what I'm talking about. If that were the case, the question would be, *"How intimate can you be with your body?"*

But I am not talking about your body. I am curious about how intimate you can be with your TRUE self. Or, with your own soul, if you will. Not sure about that? Then the easiest way to find this out is to …

…see how long you can maintain eye contact with another person.

The reason we have eyes, often beautifully colored and filled with seductive depth, is not to keep staring most of the day into a mobile phone or a computer screen. The reason we have eyes is …

... to give more love.

"It's all in the eyes" goes a well-known saying, and indeed, it all is. Just a bit differently than we were trained to believe. The eyes of another person can be a direct view into *our* own souls. That's why it is called "eye-gazing," which is really "I-gazing": you are looking at "I," at yourself.

The eyes of another person can be a direct view into *our* own souls.

Through the eyes of others, we can see and realize our own perfection. And through our eyes, others can realize their perfection in return. If you cannot maintain an I-gaze with someone for at least ten seconds, you are not intimate enough with yourself. And you are not intimate with other people, either; it may be challenging for you to connect with them on a deeper level.

Notice your tendencies. If you constantly avoid I-gaze with others, you need to cultivate greater intimacy with yourself. You remain disconnected from the love you already are, and from other beings. This deprives yourself of some of the beautiful flavors in life.

But there is still more to it.

I-gazing holds enormous healing power. It can heal many wounds in a very short time. It can help us to revisit our perfection, (self)love, and highest connection to the love we all already are. It can heal insecurities, self-worthiness challenges, pains from the past, and of course, our closed hearts.

It is also one of the highest, yet simplest forms of giving: offering selflessly, fearlessly, your being to mirror another's perfection. You need to challenge yourself to become more intimate with your own soul, until you no longer fear intimacy.

I have been fortunate enough to share I-gazing with people (mostly women) without any intent other than to exchange love-driven giving and self-realizing. This I-gazing could last for up to fifteen minutes, and it was incredibly fulfilling. It was like a gateway to deeper awakening, profound healing, and heart opening. It was as though we could see the unconditional love-sharing and true experience of oneness.

Yet, in a "normal" life, most of the time we avoid eye contact. We are driven by external programming and social, cultural, and religious beliefs, and blocked by minds full of crap, instead of acting from the love we already are. We don't allow any experience that we don't feel we have full control of, so we never realize what unconditional love is. Everything must be conditioned, under control, and socially "correct," instead of just opening our hearts and being filled with unconditional love, with no control and no expectations. We need to be living from the love-presence, not from fear of the future.

There is absolute perfection in giving a kind, vulnerable, truthful I-gaze. Even for a second. And if it comes with an honest smile, it can change a person's entire day, and for some people with low self-esteem, even an entire life. A truly self-intimate person is never worried about sharing eye contact and a smile. Why should giving this softness, kindness, nurturement, and healing cause worry?

Yet, I've observed, at least in Western society, a preference for being "icy," showing "pride" through "inaccessibility." Or, in somewhat better cases, an absence of presence: we are not even here, we don't exist. And then we complain we don't have any true connections with other people in our lives!

An I-gaze and a smile do not cost us anything.

And they give so much.

That's probably why I love traveling to so-called Third World countries. I found out that when it comes to heart-openness, they are, in fact, often first in the world. I had some deep and connecting I-gaze moments with an elderly man in Morocco. It was just a split-second, but it was enough to see and feel all that gathered wisdom of life, as well as all that beauty found behind that we call "suffering." From a brief look, I received so much heart-openness and wisdom, and at the same time so much strength, hope, and inner light.

And I had truly deep I-gazes with women in Myanmar. Even just a second or two was enough to receive deeply healing and nurturing energy of the highest feminine expression (very hard to find in today's Western society). In return, I gave my best and most supporting masculine presence.

I had many playful I-gazes with kids, who reminded me that, once, we were playful too—and there's no reason in the entire Universe why we couldn't be again. In return, I gave them appreciation for the playfulness of which they reminded me.

Many of those I-gazes felt highly intimate, and I was grateful and happy for that. Today's society suggests that intimacy is something to be ashamed of. How can we become intimate with our own souls again, in an environment like this? All those silly rules don't serve us. They cause more disconnection than connection.

We are here to find our hearts again, to realize the love we already are, to open to it fully, and let it flow again. But we can never do that from the closed state we have been so busy practicing and maintaining until now. Nothing will ever change on its own. We have to start with ourselves first. That's why I-gazing is always one of the most beautiful and enjoyable parts of my retreats. It is the moment in which we come back to our souls. We can again SEE how perfect, beautiful, and innocent we truly are.

Eyes can open our hearts, as well as the hearts of others, if only we allow it to happen. So, start giving others I-gazes full of love, even if you feel uncomfortable at first. Get over your fears, biases, and limiting beliefs. You are love. Nothing but pristine, infinite, radiating love.

You can get started by participating in the "Global Day of Eye Contact Sharing" at https://www.eyecontactexperiment.com/

Source: https://www.eyecontactexperiment.com/

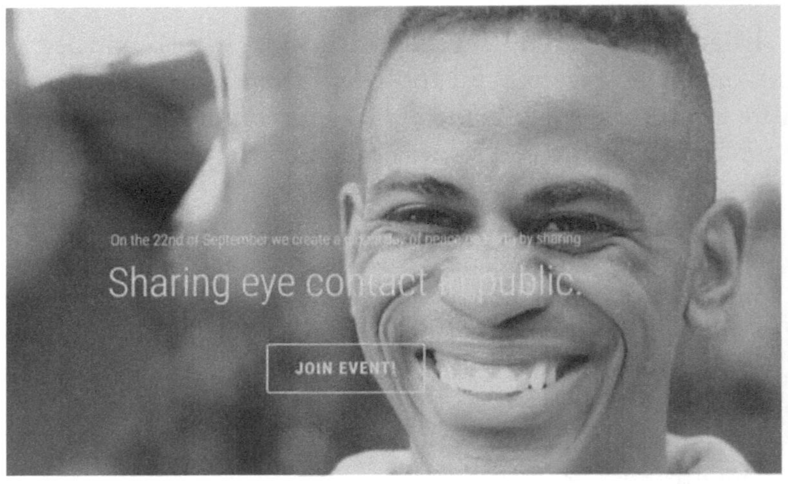

29

LIVING YOUR HIGHEST
LOVE-PURPOSE

In April of 2017, an incredible and unexpected thing happened in my life. I was invited by Jeff Walker, the ultimate online marketing superstar, to deliver an empowering and inspirational speech at his biggest event to date. An inspirational speech in front of twelve hundred people! He asked me on short notice, and I had only about three hours to get ready.

Just imagine the situation: a frighteningly huge audience. An event with the highest-caliber speakers, one rock star after another. And me, with no previous experience talking in front of so many people, hardly any time to prepare, and English as my second language. Actually, I was the one who needed some empowerment just then!

Yet, I couldn't have been more grateful. At that time, I was preparing to hold my own retreats and live events, and empowering people during them was one of the goals. So this sudden invitation felt like a gift from the Universe. It was a golden opportunity to dive in and get some practice (but, why so HUGE an audience for the very first time!).

So, I accepted, and started rapidly drafting the skeleton of my address. It is never easy to write a motivational and empowering speech, especially in a few hours. Besides, the whole thing was really emotional for me. I was filled with fear and excitement at the same time, and it was hard to focus.

So, I first had to take a few deep breaths, relax myself a bit, and then to go to a very short meditation (just a few minutes), during which I asked a question:

How can I truly GIVE myself to the audience, fully and unconditionally?

I didn't get any answer immediately. And I didn't have time to wait for one. After a few minutes, I quit the meditation and started drafting the speech. It took about half an hour for the words to finally start flowing. Then I finished writing and then spent another hour practicing the speech.

When the time came to speak, I was shaking. I felt like I had lost my voice. Yet, I mustered my courage and approached the stage as the promoter was introducing me ...

And then, in my last step before that enormous crowd of people, I finally got the answer to the question from my meditation:

It is NOT about you. It's about THEM. If you want to give truly fully and unconditionally, make EVERYTHING about them.

And that was it. That was exactly what I needed to step out of my fears and self-doubts, and get back to my full power: make it about OTHERS. I was there to GIVE as much as possible.

After that realization, I was able to totally SURRENDER to whatever was supposed to happen. With enormous relief and sudden confidence and energy, I started delivering my empowering speech. Which truly was full of power.

And it didn't just go well. It was AWESOME.

The audience was screaming, and waving, and bursting with excitement. I felt an incredibly strong connection with that huge sea of people. Thanks to their responsiveness, I had no fear. I felt like I was not doing anything, just GIVING. I was channeling power for others because it WAS about others, not me.

My reward? After the speech, many people approached me, and I made a bunch of new friends.

Give your best. Live your highest. Connect. Inspire. Touch hearts. Empower people. You are love. You have everything you need to express your highest self already. Do not allow anything or anybody to limit you. Let your opened heart and love guide you. Be courageous. Burst all your comfort-zone bubbles. Live from passion and from the true alignment with the love you already are.

And of course, the experience also gave me the boost I needed to start hosting my own retreats and live events. I started planning the first one as soon as I got back from the U.S. and delivered it in Europe later that same year.

But as always, there was another crucial lesson that I was supposed to learn from this, and as always, it took me the next few months to figure it out. And the lesson was…

THE POWER OF YOUR HEART IS BIGGER THAN YOU ARE CAPABLE OF SEEING RIGHT NOW.

And it is bigger than anything you can imagine.

Going on that stage and giving myself fully to more than a thousand people required an enormous heart-openness. Because if you want to connect with people, and if you want to truly inspire and motivate them, it can ONLY be done from heart. You must be willing to take that leap of faith—willing to open your heart unconditionally, authentically, and fearlessly for EVERYBODY in your reality. When you literally give yourself away, you experience the true power of your own heart in ways that you have never dreamed of.

Forget anything else. The power of your heart, the power of the love you are, can never be acquired by outside means. You must give to receive. You are pure love. You are perfection. You are endless, infinite power.

So, open your heart as widely as possible, and let the love flow.

Be the biggest giver of love in this Universe. Help this world to wake up into love that it has never seen before.

Live, play, and laugh.

Create.

Dance.

Let go.

Meditate.

And mainly:

GIVE.

Give as much, as you can—because you already have more than enough for yourself. Live your highest purpose. The purpose of LOVE.

I love you all.

PART III: QUESTIONS & ANSWERS

Q: *I love the idea of coming back to the love I already am. And then start living from that love and giving others. However, it somehow sounds very challenging in "daily reality."*

Yes, it does take some time. And, especially, intention and deliberateness.

So, first of all, make a very deliberate intention to merge back to the love you already are—not only romantic love, but Universal love. Make this a very clear internal goal, to align to your highest potential of love to your highest energy and state of love. Resolve to live from that love, rather than from lack and struggle, and hurdles, and hardship. Nothing will ever start moving if the intention is not there and if it is not strong enough. Be very deliberate in that. You have been seeking the home of unconditional love most of your life anyway, even if you weren't aware of it. Now you are very conscious of it, perhaps, for the first time in your life. So make this your priority. Say it to yourself: *I want to merge with the highest levels of love I can experience.*

Then, you need to have faith and conviction! The stronger you build the conviction that you are nothing but love, the faster you will align with that truth, and the faster you will be able to cut through the noise of "daily reality." Keep hold of that conviction of being nothing but love every day, even in the most challenging situations. Feel the power of that conviction. Live from that power.

And have faith in love. Let go of everything that suggests otherwise, that goes against that faith. You are love! So do not let your mind tell you otherwise. Do not listen to your mind.

Live from your heart. Mind needs to be the tool for your heart, not the other way around, as is common in our society. Feel the conviction of your heart, and keep training your faith in that conviction until it becomes reality.

Soon, the vibration of love will become stronger and stronger, until it will be the main vibration in your day. Even if it takes a few years to get to that point, it will be worth it. Don't forget, we have been heavily programmed with so many false and limiting and lack beliefs. It takes some time and a lot of intention to get rid of that nonsense and regress back to heart, where our true power is.

Q: *I somehow feel guilty about the whole idea of wanting to be nothing but love. Why is that?*

In our society, we have been brainwashed about what is supposed to be "right" to want and what is "wrong" to want. We think we have freedom of choice, but that's perhaps only as a consumer. As a human being, there are far too many subliminal programs of what we are "allowed" to want and what is perceived as "appropriate" to want. These are just subconscious suggestions from which you want to free yourself. These prevailing dogmas are based on false judgments, and they are used to manipulate people into feeling guilt whenever they want something other than the "social norm." You are love. Nothing but love. So stop worrying about what other people think. Listen to your heart only. Your heart is true. The social matrix is not. Stop being hemmed in by this false construct.

How? Start by giving yourself permission: to live in love beyond constraints.

... to be free of all the musts and shoulds.

... to break from inhibitions meant to make others feel more secure.

... to live from heart, not mind and reasoning.

... to want depth of (self)intimacy beyond what you have ever experienced.

... to want authentic connections.

... to live outside of social dogmas and judgments.

These things are not selfish. What is selfish is NOT to give yourself permission to want this and strive to be your highest potential of love. Thus, not giving and spreading love. Thus, staying small. Thus, not inspiring people and helping them to open their hearts too. Thus, not being a leading example.

If you give yourself the permission to WANT all of this, you create a desire driven by a strong intention. And the Universe will start aligning your life toward that intention: to align with your highest self.

What are you aligned with? Make your choice. And stay very persistent with that choice. Do not flinch an inch.

Q: *I try to live from love, but whenever I do, I feel too vulnerable.*

We can only feel vulnerable if we expect something in return.

If we say we live from unconditional love but at the same time expect other people to validate us for it positively, admire us for it, or give that love back, then we are not living from the source I am talking about. In that case, you are living from a neediness, and your own highly personal and often ego-driven ideas of what an unconditional love should look like. You created that neediness because you created a lack of belief in the first place. So now you are trying to compensate for that doubt. You are compensating, covering up. It is not necessarily a bad thing, but because it is not authentic, because it still comes from a place of neediness and wantingness, then it feels vulnerable.

But living fully from the source of the love you already are feels just the opposite: very empowering. Yes, there can still be feelings of vulnerability, but if you keep your heart opened, you realize that those feelings serve to transcend your limiting beliefs and to drop you even deeper into your heart. So, paradoxically, what looks like vulnerability at first glance is the most direct means to higher and higher levels of heart-driven empowerment.

Keep your conviction, keep your heart opened; do not worry about being vulnerable—just let it go. And see what will happen. It might not be comfortable at first, but you will notice SOMETHING is happening, SOMETHING is changing, SOMEHOW you are going deeper and deeper, and that vulnerability all of sudden doesn't feel that bad anymore. If you keep your heart opened, you will start welcoming that feeling of vulnerability more and more, as you will start realizing that it is a very direct gate to incredible authenticity (trying to cover up or suppress feelings of vulnerability is the direct opposite of authenticity). And that authenticity will start opening you to more and more Universal, infinite (self)love, (self)connection and (self)intimacy.

Q: *I feel like I am giving a lot of love but not receiving any in return.*

On the level of being an individual identity, you can NOT be giving a lot of unconditional love without receiving any in return. If you are truly aligned to your highest potential of the love you already are, that process of giving is a process of receiving at the same time.

You are simply channeling that high state of love for others. And because it is being channeled *through* you, you are receiving it at the same time. You cannot be channeling something without being a receiver of it first. So you are both a giver and a receiver.

Failing to grasp this may come from having expectations, making conditions around your ideas of unconditional love, coming from a place of neediness, coming from a place of doubt, and giving all your power to "permissions slips," instead of to yourself.

Just imagine: What would your life look like if you started delivering all the power you are giving to others to yourself?

There is no single reason why you couldn't and shouldn't be doing this. You already are love. And that means an infinite power. You already represent all that infinite power.

Make an intentional effort to drop your mind full of limiting self-beliefs and realign with your heart again. That's where that passion and power can be ignited; that's where you can start taking all that power back.

Never mind what people think. Don't worry about others feeling insecure about your priorities. You are meant to lead by example, to inspire them to start getting their power back too. So, let yourself be that infinite love again. Then you can be that light and inspiration, and sparkle for others.

You are love. You are here to be that love, to live that love, and to give that love.

YOUR NEXT LOVE-STEP

Congratulations! You DID IT! :-)

You've just finished the book. I'm so proud of you!

And I can promise you that very soon you'll be ready to welcome an incredible and magical flow of love into your life - like never before!

But before that...

How about we continue on this love-journey TOGETHER just for a little bit longer?

Here's what I mean:

I have prepared an amazing 'You Are Love' Online Course for you. It includes practical examples of the whole 'You Are Love' process, professionally recorded meditations (including netti-netti), and 3 very powerful, heart-centered videos.

This course is normally worth $279 USD, but because I really want you to grow towards the highest love-experience possible, for now I'm giving it to you completely for FREE. (Note: This can change in the near future).

So, what I'm inviting you to do right now, is to just go to www.YouAreLoveBook.com/love.

I promise that you'll love what you'll find there (including an additional 'secret' chapter of the book!). It'll tremendously speed up your results with the 'You Are Love' process.

Just go to www.YouAreLoveBook.com/love right now - see you there!

Welcome and START HERE!

STEP #1:
Letting Go

How To LET GO:
Case Study

*Join me now in this FREE 'You Are Love'
Online Course at www.YouAreLoveBook.com/love*

REVIEW REQUEST

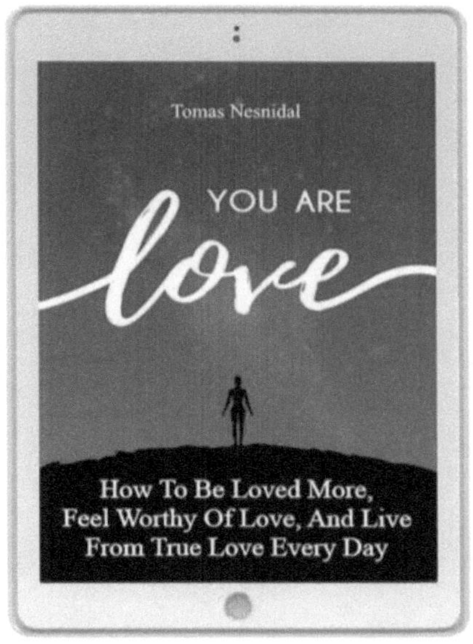

Most of us don't spend the time to review items we like. We only write reviews when we are dissatisfied. In reality, the best way to get more good products out there is to let people know that you are happy with them. What you might not know is how valuable even a one-sentence review is to an author. It is like gold. Most authors read every review. I would go as far as to say that reviews are more valuable than sales for each book. If this book helped you, and I hope it has, would you please leave me an honest review on Amazon?

Reviews: <u>You Are Love on Amazon</u>